Murder In Seal Chart

John Brookland

BB
BitzaBooks

First published in UK 2025
by bitzabooks.co.uk

ISBN: 978-1068645068
Also available as an Ebook.

All the characters are real, and no invented persons or story-lines have been included, but some of the dialogue and scenes have been dramatised.

A CIP catalogue record for this book is available from the British Library.

To Debbie for her support

Contents

Dedication v

1 AUTHOR'S NOTE 1
2 PROLOGUE 3
3 48 HOURS AFTER THE MURDER 7
4 DAY OF MURDER 15
5 TUESDAY 31
6 THE INQUEST 49
7 USELESS CLUES & WASTED TIME 71
8 THE LUARD TRAGEDY 85
9 A YEAR LATER – AN ARREST 113
10 THE AFTERMATH 126
11 WHODUNNIT? 135
12 WHO WAS EDWIN FOWLE? 139
13 BIBLIOGRAPHY 144
ABOUT THE AUTHOR 148
THE EDWARDIAN DETECTIVE EDWIN FOWLE SERIES 150

1

AUTHOR'S NOTE

The 1908 unsolved murder of Caroline Luard has been the subject of extensive writing over the decades, characterized by enduring mystery and intrigue. Given this widespread coverage, one might question the necessity of another book on the topic. While I do not claim to have discovered new evidence that will definitively solve the case, I do offer my own reflections at the conclusion of the book. This narrative delves more deeply into the intrigue, mayhem and consequences it had for the police and the local community, also the social and political upheaval it caused and more importantly the devastation of the Luard family.

This publication is the third volume in The Edwardian Detective Edwin Fowle Series, which chronicles his murder investigations during his tenure as head of the Kent County Constabulary detective department which happened to include the Luard case. Previous accounts have oddly overlooked his contribution, focusing instead on Scotland Yard, which had minimal involvement in the case. This oversight can be attributed to a romanticized view of the "Yard" by many writers and a lack of understanding regarding the organizational structure and operations of the Kent Force at the time. In order to do justice to Detective Inspector Edwin

Fowle and his colleagues, this narrative is written on their behalf and from the perspective of the real lead investigating officer.

2

PROLOGUE

Caroline Mary Luard 1850-1908

On the fine summer afternoon of 24 August 1908 a dreadful murder was committed near the picturesque Kentish village of Ightham in a spot known locally as Seal Chart, two miles west of the village and five miles east of Sevenoaks, nestled in a quiet corner of the Garden of England. The murder was described by the local *Sevenoaks Chronicle* newspaper as "not only the most sensational crime of the age, but one of the most mysterious that sent a thrill of horror through the whole country" It threw the community into disarray and had repercussions way beyond the actual murder including the devastation of the Luard family.

In 1908, the village was and still is, full of ancient half-timbered houses overlooked by a medieval church and surrounded by large country houses and estates such as Ightham Court, Ightham Mote, Barham Court and St Clere. These housed peers, clergy, judiciary and retired military gentlemen who made up the cream of County society, although these are long gone. The area was a secluded place, with few interests outside its own borders. Everybody knew everybody else and everyone knew their place. Labourers saluted generals and Lords, while Justices of the Peace socialised with the doctors and the clergy, and villagers gossiped the doings of the gentry. It had been like this for centuries, but the killing of a woman of high social position, or "one of their own," without apparent motive in broad daylight on a summer afternoon on private property suddenly blighted their idyllic milieu and unsettled them.

Their ire turned towards what they perceived as the "pests infesting the countryside" referring to the nuisance and threat caused by the massive influx of poor Londoners, economic vagrants, gypsies and thieves who arrived in the spring and summer looking for seasonal work, particularly for the six-week long hop and apple picking season. Many lived rough in the woods and fields often trespassing on the gentry property. It was a topic that had been regularly discussed at their dinner parties and had festered under the surface for a long time.

The police were under pressure from the beginning to solve the crime quickly and came under great criticism but were hindered by many limitations. Their main problem was that they had no prime suspect, witnesses, motive, murder weapon or forensics. They were also hampered by a total lack of technological and forensic assets that modern policing enjoy. Transport and adequate communication was an improvised affair with only a few Kent police stations linked to the telephone; village police stations were only connected in 1925, so only telegram, post office runners or hand delivery was available to them. Transport was by horseback, train, hired cab, or hitching lifts with only 130 police bicycles in the County mainly used by village bobbies. Superintendents had the luxury of a pony and trap with a driver, a step up from the dog carts they previously used, but most constables completed their beat on foot. These drawbacks made it impossible to arrive at crime scenes quickly or to relay or receive urgent messages. None of these difficulties though curbed the determination of Det. Inspector Edwin Fowle and his detectives to crack the case.

Edwin Fowle was a much respected and renowned officer with a natural aptitude for detective work. He was a stickler for correct police procedure and record keeping and his superiors and the judiciary were complimentary of the way he prepared cases for court, few of which failed to get a prosecution. In his twelve years as a detective Edwin had an unrivalled record of success having investigated many high profile murder cases receiving many commendations plus a coveted police merit medal. Two of the more sensational ones were the 1901 Tonbridge Murder when a seven-year-old girl was abducted, raped and murdered on New Year's Eve and the 1905 Tenterden Murder when an Algerian street hawker had his throat cut in a field in the hamlet of St Michaels; accounts of both these murders can be found in my Detective Edwin Fowle Series. His full profile can be found at the end of the book. But was this case going to be one of his most challenging?

3

48 HOURS AFTER THE MURDER

Ightham Knoll

On the afternoon of Wednesday 26 August 1908, thirty-six-year-old Detective Inspector Edwin Fowle was seated at a long table covered in a red tablecloth in the oak panelled dining room of an unpretentious house with half-timbered gables and red tiled walls named Ightham Knoll. It was nestled in eight acres of ground a little beyond the quaint Sir Jeffrey Amherst tavern, a favourite watering hole of the West Kent Foxhounds meet. It was named thus as it stood on a prominence in a clearing in the dense pine and oak woods which in summer had a dense undergrowth of bramble and bracken. The area was known by the local population as Seal Chart, Seal being the name of one of the nearby villages some four miles from Sevenoaks. Ightham Knoll had been the rented residence of Major-General Charles Edward Luard R.E., F.R.G.S, J.P. and his wife Caroline since his retirement in 1887.

Edwin was there to take part in an inquest and awaiting the arrival of the District Coroner Thomas Buss, a man Edwin knew well as they had worked together on many murder and suspicious death cases. It was an unusual venue for such an official inquiry, particularly when the body of the victim was still lying in the bedroom above his head. He was more accustomed to attending them in local taverns, hotels, council halls and churches but never in the dining room of a rather grand private house and never under the circumstances he was presently witnessing. But then, everything that had occurred over the last two days had been unusual and in his twelve years as a detective he had never experienced anything quite like it.

The Luards were familiar and popular figures in the area and had collected a legion of rich and influential friends through his duties as a JP and had joined the ranks of the county set. For this reason Edwin's inquiry was already proving a diplomatic nightmare and he had to tread very carefully. The Luards were surrounded by many prominent people. Next door was the Frankfield Estate home to eighty-year-old retired stockbroker Horace Wilkinson and his wife Annie. Edwin was aware that he was terminally ill and most famous for owning Oliver Cromwell's embalmed head, which he inherited from his father Josiah Wilkinson in 1822 who bought it for £100. Another close friend was sixty-three-year-old Colonel Charles Warde late of the West Kent Yeomanry. He was the MP for the Medway Constituency and lived on the grand Barham Court Estate outside the village of Teston. But his closest friend was his brother fifty-eight-year-old Lt Col. Henry Murray Ashley Warde late of the 19th Hussars who happened to be the Chief Constable of Kent and Edwin's boss, which was already causing Edwin some headaches.

Edwin stared out of one of the mullioned bay windows in an exhaustion induced trance caused by forty-eight hours on duty with little sleep. He was having difficulty keeping awake and was being lulled further by the sound of gently ticking clocks. He admired the large expanse of neat lawn and well stocked colourful flowerbeds against the blue sky and trying to relax. But it was not a peaceful scene due to the general commotion of orders being shouted, loud conversations and the irritating noise of motor car engines. There were groups of exhausted uniformed colleagues who had searched the whole area all through Monday night into Tuesday in torrential rain in a desperate bid to find elusive evidence and he was thankful he had not been one of them. The unseasonable weather of heavy rain and gales, which had lasted for days following a drought, had hampered their search but today it had dawned clear.

Earlier that morning he had watched the ever-industrious Sergeant Paramour of the Sevenoaks police arranging the seating with the help of some of his men and the morose house staff, removing most of the furniture and valuables and stripping every room in the house to gather an assortment of chairs which had been positioned to form the resemblance of a courtroom. He had wandered the hallways while this was occurring admiring the paintings and the large collection of native masks, shields and spears adorning the walls which the General had obviously collected on his postings. Apparently he had served in Gibraltar, Bermuda, Corfu and Natal in South Africa where he had surveyed and sketched the country in which General Buller's army afterwards fought his fiercest battles.

His gaze drifted to a portrait of the General dressed in his scarlet uniform of the Royal Engineers with his medals proudly displayed on his chest. Below it was a photograph of two smiling boys, his two sons, Charles and Eric. Eric had died from fever while serving with the Queen's Own Royal West Kent Regiment in Somaliland, but Charles Elmhirst was presently stationed in Natal, South Africa, a Captain in the King's African rifles. He had survived a serious injury in the battle of Abassi and received a D.S.O.

Edwin was shaken out of his indolence as more people began to enter the room. These were the seventeen strong jury summoned from nearby villages, dressed as smartly as was possible under their varying financial circumstances. They had been assigned the bay window seat and other chairs in front of the window with their backs to the garden probably purposely to avoid them being distracted by the goings on outside. He could imagine how their wives and mothers had fussed over them to ensure that they did not let down the family reputation on such an important occasion. Most of them were obviously overawed about being in such a house which in normal circumstances they would never have been invited into. Earlier they had been led in a sombre procession up the stairs to view the body in the bedroom and had returned rather subdued as would be expected. He felt sorry for them as he would bet anything that the inquest, on past performances, would be protracted and probably drag on for weeks keeping them away from their work.

He could now see Superintendent Albert Taylor, whom, again, he had worked many cases with, chatting in the hallway to his boss the Chief Constable of Warde. In many respects Edwin was lucky as the detective department was autonomous and only answerable to him, but sometimes Edwin was frustrated when he interfered as was happening in this case. Albert Taylor was a rather flamboyant character, tall, thin and in his early sixties with an extravagant handlebar moustache and whiskers. He was to retire in three years after a long successful career to be replaced by the newly promoted Edwin. But that was the future. Each of the twelve Kent police divisions had a superintendent in charge, the highest uniformed rank at the time, and Albert was head of the Sevenoaks Division within whose jurisdiction the murder had occurred.

Once the superintendent had finished his discussion, a smartly dressed man approached the Chief Constable. He was Chief Inspector James Scott of Scotland Yard who had been sent down from London at the request of Warde as a consultant and had arrived that morning to great interest from the press. He was known as "a man of few words, but of great experience." The man had a modest handlebar moustache with goatee beard and was dressed in an expensive looking suit with waistcoat and a spotted tie. Edwin had to admit he looked very dapper, but then he was from London.

Edwin eyed the Yard man with just a pinch of resentment because he was already being viewed as some kind of saviour which had piqued a bit of jealousy from Edwin who felt that being an experienced and successful detective of twelve years standing himself, he had the investigation well in hand and did not need outside help. He felt his authority and role on the case had been usurped somewhat before he had had the chance to fully investigate. He realised deep down that the request was more of a face-saving exercise should the local force fail to solve the case. With the Yard present they could easily be blamed on the basis that if "Scotland Yard cannot solve it who can." Provisional police officers countrywide had historically a natural antipathy towards London detectives muscling in on their patches invited or not and this was why many had created their own detective departments.

He looked round the table. Opposite him were two empty chairs for the coroner and his assistant who would sit with their backs to the fireplace and a chair to the right for the witnesses. Facing the Coroner and on Edwin's left would be Warde, and on his left Scott. Sitting on the right side of Edwin would be Superintendent Taylor and Major Lafone, the Deputy Chief. This line up only exemplified the importance attached to the case but the presence of so many high-ranking officers made Edwin somewhat uncomfortable and the whole scenario was rather surreal. Some were already querying the hands-on presence of Warde in the case as a clash of interest with him being a great friend of the Luard family and other upper-class notables involved.

Edwin had realised immediately that the case would be treated as sensational, and he had been proved right; but it was also proving to be a bit of a circus particularly in regard to the behaviour of the huge press contingent now making themselves a noisy nuisance outside. He could not believe how quickly the press had got hold of the story unaware that a *Chronicle* correspondent, Foster MacAdam, had achieved a scoop and had immediately put the story on the wires to press agencies in London and elsewhere. He had never been a fan of the press in any of its guises. In his opinion they were intrusive, interfering, prone to exaggerate, and sensationalise, embellish and invent stories and were a general blimming nuisance.

It was a habit that he had acquired when first becoming a detective and read the General Orders which stipulated that "a detective should avoid everything likely to lead to their identity" requiring him to preserve his anonymity at all costs in order to be able to execute his duties and "should give every possible assistance to the police in the several divisions, keeping as much as possible out of the witness box themselves." It always made Edwin smile when he thought back to those early days and the naivety of the General Orders particularly the bit "Detective officers, when on duty, should not, unless absolutely necessary, be seen in company with officers in uniform, nor should they be seen in police vehicles, nor in any situation likely to cause suspicion that they are connected with the Constabulary. They should not salute." He often wondered whether he was a spy or a police officer, but he always liked the bit about not saluting. It was fine not to appear in the witness box but totally impractical. His job description was to obtain "information and evidence which he should place in the hands of divisional superintendents to work on, rather than appear in court himself" but it rarely worked that way. During his career he had dealt with scores of high-profile cases and could not avoid court appearances and reluctantly found his name in newspaper coverage all the time.

A jostling scrum of thirty plus members of the press intent on witnessing the inquest had gathered early that morning at the gate of the Knoll in anticipation. They had much to their indignation been barred from entering due to the lack of space. This had caused a furore and police constables had been assigned to keep them at bay while negotiations took place. They constantly badgered the two officers guarding the gate for information, and whenever they were pushed back to allow entry to a carriage, they stared keenly at the occupants and bulbs flashed.

Many had already begun to rebel against the hearing being held behind "closed doors" when such inquiries were by law open to anyone. It was as though there was an attempt to shroud it in secrecy. Officers were guarding the estate gates and patrolling the woods and fields to repel over keen reporters who were trying to use footpaths that meandered the woodland around the house to circumvent the police blockade. He could hear Albert and Warde discussing the situation and it appeared that due to the cramped venue, only six reporters were going to be allowed in. They were unaware of this at the moment, and he hoped it wasn't going to be him who had to face them when they were made aware of the decision.

When Thomas Buss the Coroner finally arrived he had to push his way through the throng with questions being shouted from all directions. Sergeant Paramour announced his arrival, and he bustles into the room and acknowledged everyone as they stood. The jury were then sworn in, and the inquest was finally ready to get underway. Paramour stood at the dining room door and had the duty of calling in the witnesses and the coroner turned to him and indicated to call the first one.

4

DAY OF MURDER

Det. Insp. Edwin Fowle, Supt. Albert Taylor, Det. C/Inspector James Scott at the Luard murder scene 1908

Alamy Image

On the afternoon of 24 August, General Charles Luard was patiently waiting outside the house with his faithful Irish terrier Sergeant for his wife Caroline to join him, while keeping an eye on his pocket watch as he was mindful that they were expecting the arrival of a guest for afternoon tea at 4.30pm and it was already 2.30pm. He was a keen golfer and a member of the nearby Godden Green golf club and he had arranged to pick up some of his clubs to take with them for their impending short holiday in Cumberland to visit Caroline's extremely wealthy brother. He owned some coal mines and lived in Armathwaite Hall, a spectacular sixteenth century building on the shores of Bassenthwaite Lake which he acquired in 1880 and totally refurbished and extended. Caroline had offered to walk part of the way with him as it was such a pleasant afternoon.

He had been married to Caroline for thirty-three years and knew it was not necessary to hurry her; she would be there in her own time. He smiled to himself musing what a lucky man he was as their marriage in 1875 had been a close-run thing. She was the youngest daughter of Thomas and Georgina Hartley of Gillfoot, Egremont in Dumfries on the edge of the Lake District National Park in Cumberland. The landed gentry Hartley family had reservations that she was marrying below her status. He could never understand why as he was proud of his lineage being a member of one of the Huguenots families who came to England in 1685 and also of Scottish descent having been born in Edinburgh on October 13, 1839. The family seat since 1754 was Blyborough Hall in Lincolnshire and the family menfolk had for generations either served in the army, most rising to high rank, or diversely had taken the cloth.

Charles's father was Major Robert Luard Selby of the Royal Artillery who before his death in 1880 had lived at Ightham Mote, a famous house and estate just a few miles from where Charles lived now. His mother was a Colonel's daughter of landed gentry but unfortunately died when Charles was only eleven. His father remarried to a widowed heiress named Marianne Bigge nee Selby who had two teenage children. The couple had two more children giving Charles four step and half brothers and sisters who all remained close. She had inherited Ightham Mote which had been in the Selby family for three hundred years so in order to continue this connection they changed their surname to Luard-Selby. Charles had happy memories of the house and was the reason he chose to live near it after his retirement. When his father died, Marianne moved out, rented it and finally sold it in 1889 to Sir Thomas Colyer-Ferguson. Although not in Luard hands when Charles returned to the area he remained a regular visitor to the house.

He was thinking of stepping back inside when she appeared wearing a plaid skirt and white silk blouse topped with a straw hat, 'Come on Daisy time is getting on,' he said using the family pet name for her which referred to her favourite flower. They set off, the General looking every bit the quintessential Edwardian country squire with his military bearing, iron grey hair, white moustache and walking stick and dressed in tweeds. Sergeant his faithful dog was trotting in front of them, nose to the ground, searching out trails as all country dogs like to do. They walked along a well-worn path through the bracken busily chatting arm in arm at one point. Caroline told her husband that she wouldn't go all the way but stop off at her favourite haunt, a summerhouse named La Casa belonging to their neighbours the Wilkinsons. There was a magnificent view from the veranda and on a clear day the villages of Wrotham and Ightham and local landmarks such as Trosley Towers and Blue Bell Hill were easily visible, plus the undulating green countryside and golden cornfields. Because of their close friendship the Luards had free movement over their estate.

Forty years before when the Wilkinsons moved from Croydon, Mr Wilkinson built a wooden summerhouse at his wife's request and it was constructed on the highest part of the estate, a promontory facing south west, but in 1896 it burned down and was replaced with the a substantial bungalow of stuccoed walls and shingled roof with a small stable and a well. It was named La Casa and consisted of six rooms, including three bedrooms and a veranda built on piles to compensate for the steep incline to give it a splendid view over a nearby pond. It was kept locked when not in use and a key was available from the coachman's cottage.

Mrs Wilkinson and her two daughters would often stay in it for two weeks in the summer and it was also often used for their visiting guests. During the previous two years only the occasional afternoon tea had been held there. It stood in half an acre of garden which had recently been neglected giving the place an aura of abandonment and it had been recently broken into. It was situated on the edge of a thick pine and fir wood. Within a few hundred yards of the Casa was a cottage used as a convalescent home for destitute children from London slums operated by one of Annie's daughters and which Caroline often visited.

When they reached a wicket gate at 3pm that led into the Wilkinson estate, Caroline said she would head home as it was still another half hour walk to the golf course and she needed to get back for their guest but would stop off for a few moments at the Casa on her way, which was just a slight detour, to take in the view. She was quite happy to wander the woodland paths alone although her husband was always telling her to beware of the many itinerants and tramps. He gave her a peck on the cheek and suggested she take Sergeant, but Caroline said he would get bored waiting for her and would enjoy the long walk to the golf club. They waved to each other and the General continued across a public road and down through a wood that led to the golf club where he passed Kemp the green-keeper and gave him a wave before entering the club house to retrieve his clubs. He then decided he would head home along Stone Street, a slightly quicker route than using the woodland footpaths.

***

Alice Mary Stewart and her husband Frank, a retired Minister, rented Bats Wood Cottage in Ightham and had only recently arrived to spend the summer months. As was etiquette at the time she wanted to make a courtesy call on the Luards to introduce herself. She had visited the house back in June, but they were away, so she had left a calling card. Unfortunately this was mislaid so it was a while before the mix up was noticed which upset her, but eventually she received an invitation to tea on Monday afternoon 24 September. Her husband was unable to attend that day, so not wanting to miss out again she went there on her own and arrived at twenty minutes past four. She was shown into the drawing room by the parlour maid Harriet Huish and told that the General would be with her shortly.

He arrived five minutes afterwards and was informed by the cook that his wife had not arrived back and she wasn't sure what to do about the tea. He told her to wait for a while and headed into the drawing room and greeted Alice.

"Very nice to meet you Mrs Stewart. I am sorry Mrs Luard is not here yet. She is out on a walk but appears to have been delayed. I'm sure she will be back soon.'

Charles told Alice to sit and then he did the same, but he had never been that comfortable at small talk with new guests having always left that to his wife.

'I'm sure she won't be long,' he repeated, 'We'll wait a few minutes before having tea.'

After waiting about five minutes, he called for the maid, 'Harriet can you please serve tea now and see if anyone has seen Mrs Luard.'

'Yes sir,' said Harriet quickly leaving the room.

Charles did his best to keep the conversation going but by the time they had finished tea his wife had not arrived back. He was getting concerned as it was almost unheard of for her to be so rude as not to attend an appointment. He pulled out his pocket watch and stared at it.

'I'm sorry Mrs Stewart but this is really out of character for my wife and I must admit I'm worried that something may have happened to her. I had better go and look for her.'

'I fully understand, General. I shall accompany you if I may in case you require help.'

'That is very kind of you, but only if you wish.'

He called Sergeant who came trotting up the corridor from the kitchen and led the two out of the house and headed up the path that his wife would have used to return to the house, but there was still no sign of her. It was now 5.15pm and as they reached the top of the hill the General turned to Mrs Stewart and said, 'You had better wait here and I will go on ahead and see if I can find her.'

'Are you sure General, I can easily accompany you?'

'No my dear there is no need for both of us to continue.'

'I must admit that I need to meet another friend.'

'That's fine. Off you go and thank you for your help. Again I can only apologise and we must make another appointment.'

'That's quite alright. I hope you find Mrs Luard.'

'So do I madam.'

He walked on with Sergeant scampering on ahead.

'Find your mistress, Sergeant. Find her,' he shouted to the dog.

He strode as quickly as he was able through the thick woodland heading for the Casa, her intended destination. He was unable to see that far ahead due to the thick foliage but as he neared the summerhouse he could glimpse Sergeant through the trees standing on the veranda barking and staring at something. As he got closer he could see a figure prone on the floor and realised it was Caroline. He initially thought she had fainted or fallen. He called out to her as he rushed up the steps and could see Sergeant licking her face. He pulled him away and knelt down.

He gasped at the sight of the blood that was seeping from her head. At first he could not take in what he was seeing. His emotions then overwhelmed him and he began to wail and cried out her name repeatedly and Sergeant also howled recognising his master's distress. Eventually his military training allowed him to take control as any old soldier would. Having checked for a pulse and ascertained she was dead, there was nothing else he could do. He had a quick look round to see if anyone was about to no avail. What to do he thought. He then took a minute to weigh up his options and decided to head for the nearest cottage which was the home of the Frankfield estate coachman separated from the Casa by woodland and a meadow about halfway to the Wilkinson house. He had to drag himself away not wanting to leave her alone, but there was no other option. Even though sixty-seven years old he was reasonably fit for his age and made a good but stumbling pace down the steep hill and through the overshadowing pine trees.

He finally reached the cottage and staggered into the front garden at about 5.30pm hoping someone was at home. He was now gasping for breath and shouted for help. Annie Wickham, the coachman's wife, was in the kitchen busily doing chores when she heard the commotion. She did not recognise the anguished voice initially and when she hurried outside was surprised to find the General. She knew something serious must have happened as he looked as white as death with his face drawn and twisted with agony.

'Whatever can be the matter sir? she inquired, 'It seems something terrible has happened to you.'

The General, out of breath, was almost unable to respond but gasped 'Is your husband here madam? I need your husband quickly.'

'I'm afraid not sir. He is at work at the farmhouse. Is there anything I can do? Would you like a drink or a sit down?'

'No, no, thank you. I just need your husband urgently.'

'I expect you'll find him in the stable yard. Are you sure I cannot do something to help sir.'

'No thank you. I will find your husband.'

With that he stumbled on watched by an alarmed and puzzled Annie.

He finally reached the Frankfield farmhouse in a state of collapse and entered the yard still crying for help. Fred Wickham was cleaning in the harness room quietly singing to himself. When he heard the shouting he rushed out to find the General staggering round the yard and rushed over to him, grabbing him round the waist to support him. At first he thought the General had been attacked or had fallen and could not make out what he was trying to communicate to him.

'What on earth is the matter,' he shouted, but the General was too exhausted to speak coherently although he attempted to. Finally he said, 'Dead. Shot, I tell you!'

'Sorry Sir, what are you talking about? Whose dead?' Fred asked worriedly.

'My wife is dead. Shot, can't you understand damn you.'

'Your wife!' exclaimed Fred. 'Are you sure sir?'

'Of course I'm sure.'

'Where is she?

'At the Casa. You must help me,' pleaded the General.

A stable lad appeared wondering what all the shouting was about. Fred called to the lad.

'Quick lad. Go to the house and get some brandy and tell Mr Harding to get here double quick. The General is in trouble'

He aided him into the harness room and sat him on a box. The stable lad rushed off to find Harding the butler at the house. He arrived with the brandy and was shocked to find the General "completely broken, grief- stricken and near to collapse." Fred encouraged him to drink the brandy, but he refused, and the two men had great trouble understanding what had happened to him as he was "crying and groaning all the while." At one point Harding heard him say "My wife is dead at the Casa."

The shocked Harding asked, 'Are you sure she has not fainted?'

The General shouted, 'No damn it, much worse than that. You must come with me, now.'

All that they could establish was that something terrible had befallen his wife at the Casa. Harding turned to Fred and said, 'I had better get up to there to see what has happened while you wait with the General and organise more help.'

'No, 'the General commanded, 'you must take me back with you. I cannot leave her there alone any longer.'

Harding turned to Fred, 'You had better come with me.'

'Shouldn't we call the police?'

'Not yet. Who knows what we are going to find. Best wait until we know we need them.'

The two men set off, but it was slow progress as the General was physically and mentally worn out. They walked fifty yards or so then had to stop for him to get his breath and all the time he was groaning and crying in distress. At one-point Harding heard him say "the brutes; they have killed her." Harding then realised for the first time how serious the situation was and tried to hurry on. All this time Sergeant had been running backwards and forwards trying to hurry them, and as they neared, he rushed off ahead and up onto the veranda sitting next to his mistress.

The General rushed to his wife's body and collapsed down next to her and took her hand in his and with his other hand stroked her bloodied forehead. When Harding and Wickham reached the body they gasped and quickly ascertained she was dead.

'God dammit, she really has been shot!' shouted Harding.

He turned to Fred, 'Quick as you can, go and get the police and a doctor.'

Wickham ran down the path, but they had a long wait until help arrived. Harding attempted to console the distressed General with little success. It wasn't long before news of a tragedy at the Casa reached the ears of Reverend Scott of nearby St. Lawrence's Church, a close friend of the Luards. He rushed to the scene to see if he could give any assistance, not knowing what to expect and was shocked at what he found. He did his best to placate his friend and convince him to return to the Knoll while the officials did what needed to be done.

Local doctor Percival A Mansfield, received a telephone call telling him that a "woman" had been found dead in the woods on the Frankfield estate. He received few details and hadn't been informed who the woman was. On arrival at the Frankfield estate he was directed to the Casa, not arriving until 7.40pm. He was startled when he got there, to see Caroline Luard lying on her front with her head in a pool of blood.

***

Foster McAdam was an enterprising journalist who always had his ear to the ground and was ready to go the extra mile to get ahead of the competition and obtain the best stories for his newspaper the *Sevenoaks Chronicle,* the leading rag in town. He got wind early on about a serious and sensational incident on the Frankfield estate but was unaware at the time of how big this story was to be. He was familiar with the area and knew the quickest route was to drive to St Lawrence School near the church where he parked his car and passed through a gateway and along a track that led up a steep coombe lined with pine trees to the estate. At the top and a few yards to the right stood the Casa. He was aware of the building but had never visited it before being on private property. He was in a heightened state of excitement hoping to be the first and only reporter to reach the scene, a real scoop. As he approached he saw a man on the veranda crouching over something which made him duck down. He wasn't sure what to do but then the man stood up and he recognised him as Dr Mansfield, who he knew well. Relieved he approached calling out to the doctor who turned.

'Oh it's you Foster. How on earth did you get here? The police haven't arrived yet.'

'My lucky day then. What we got, doc?'

'I'm not sure I should tell you. The police will not be best pleased if you are still here when they arrive.'

'The police? Why are they coming?'

Foster stepped onto the veranda and although he had seen a few bodies in his line of work he was still shocked. He was immediately revolted by the smell of blood mixed with that of a pool of vomit near her head.

'Oh my God, is that who I think it is?' he exclaimed holding his hand to his mouth.

'Afraid so, Mrs Luard.'

'Is she dead?'

'Again, I'm sorry to say she is.'

'This is awful. What on earth has happened to her?'

'That's what I am trying to discover.'

He looked at the face down body of the woman with her legs straight out and the toes of her boots pointing towards the outer edge. He could see a copious blood pool that had seeped a foot either side of her head. It was an unreal and ghastly sight.

'Has she fainted or fallen and hit her head? Foster asked.

'Doesn't look like it,' answered the doctor.

'Don't say she's been killed, surely?'

'Could well be but I'm not saying anything at the moment, especially to you. You'd better get out of here.'

Foster took another look and quickly scribbled some notes; his eyes drawn to a large dented straw hat trimmed with blue ribbon which was lying a yard away with blood stains on the back of it. The doctor carried on examining the body and Foster hurried back to his car already formulating a story and made his way to the village of Seal Chart to discover more information.

Dr Mansfield knew that this investigation would be scrupulously evaluated and he would be required to give a detailed statement so while he awaited the police he made copious notes of the scene. He scribbled that Caroline was lying face down with her cheek to the ground. Her arms were by her side with the backs of the hands uppermost. Her feet were turned to the left pointing towards the edge of the veranda with which the body was lying in line. From the edge of the veranda to her feet was about six feet and she was lying nearer the door of the Casa than the edge of the veranda. Her head was lying in a pool of blood, and there was a large clot of vomit and a pool of blood the size of a saucer about eighteen inches from the veranda edge and a smaller clot connecting this to the blood by her head. There was a large amount of blood on her left temple. Under the body was a left-hand glove turned half inside out, and he noticed the pocket in her dress was ripped off against the grain of cloth. Her large straw hat trimmed with blue ribbon was lying a yard away with blood stains and a dent on the back of it. He stood up still trying to assimilate what he was seeing and heard someone else approaching.

***

The first police officer on the scene was Sergeant Paramour, soon followed by thirty-six-year-old local Constable John Joseph Marsh who came from his police house at 2 High Street in Seal. Both men like everyone else who were to arrive were aghast at the scene before them. Paramour immediately sent Marsh back to the Knoll to use their telephone to call for more help and to contact their boss, Superintendent Albert Taylor who received the call about the murder at 7.20pm and was the next officer to arrive, getting there at about 7.50pm. He in turn had contacted the Chief Constable realising the seriousness of the case and also that the Luards were close friends of the General and his wife which he immediately knew would complicate matters. He had ordered that all available officers were to head to the scene. The superintendent and the doctor greeted each other.

'A very shocking and sad day don't you think?' the doctor stated.

'Indeed it is. I take it that it is a murder not suicide?' The superintendent asked in reply.

'Obviously too early to tell definitely but almost certainly a murder. Shot twice in the head from close range.'

'My God, it doesn't bear thinking about. How long ago?'

The Doctor checked his watch, 'Possibly three or four hours ago I would say.'

While he awaited for more backup the superintendent, Paramour and Marsh began searching the immediate area and found the vague outlines of footprints leading from the back of the Casa to a trail of flattened and broken bracken ending at a hedge some ten or so yards away where they lost any other signs of disturbance. Returning to the Casa they searched the bracken in front of the house for any evidence. Taylor spotted the distressed General heading towards him from the direction of his house and he gave a sigh realising that Reverend Scott had not managed to keep him away. He insisted on seeing his wife again which the superintendent wasn't happy about but relented. The General was adamant he wanted his wife moved back to the Knoll but was told that couldn't be done at the moment.

As more officers arrived, Paramour delegated them to conduct a search of the surrounding woods and fields in the hope of discovering any evidence. The light was fading fast, and the superintendent made it clear that they would all be up most of the night. Officers arrived clutching their police issue lamps plus lamps and candles from the Knoll were also used to light up the veranda and summerhouse. The superintendent realised this was going to be a massive investigation and needed as much help as possible, so he contacted the adjoining Malling Division for more officers. He then put out a call for Detective Inspector Edwin Fowle. It was protocol for the divisional superintendents to immediately refer high profile complex cases requiring specialist investigation to the relatively new detective department. It had only been operating out of the force's headquarters at Wrens Court, Maidstone since 1896 and was responsible for solving serious crimes County wide.

Edwin was a founding member of the department having been the first of three detective constables on the force and had gained considerable experience in crime solving moving up the ranks to inspector. Due to other commitments he was unable to make it to the scene that evening but promised to be there first thing on Tuesday morning.

Once the doctor had completed all his investigations the body was removed into the Casa and put on a camp bed in one of the bedrooms. The General who was now more composed sat by the bed speaking to her and getting visibly upset but the doctor was unable to get him to leave. On several occasions he went to Taylor and complained that he was not happy about his wife's body remaining on the camp bed and insisted she was taken to the Knoll to complete her journey home and spend her last night in her bedroom in familiar surroundings. Taylor initially refused these heart-rending pleas informing him more work needed to be done, and photographs taken. The General continued his objections stating that he thought it was rather undignified for her to remain where she was. Finally at 9pm he agreed, but the only suitable vehicle they could find on the farm was a large fruit van.

John Kettle the farm steward arranged for it to be brought up to the Casa where it was positioned by the veranda. The body was then carried as respectably as possible on the camp bed mattress and put into the back. A rather macabre lantern lit slow procession then ensued as the General insisted leading the procession the whole way to his house by walking in front of the cart. At Ightham Knoll there was a heart-breaking scenario of the tearful staff greeting their mistress home as she was conveyed on the mattress up the stairs to her bed where the General laid her out and placed a sheet over her. Then he spent the whole night in his study writing letters and telegrams to family members and close friends across the country informing them of the tragic news while his distraught servants also kept vigil to support him and badgering him to eat and drink.

They searched painstakingly all night trying to ascertain any trail the attacker made have left, a dropped cigarette, torn clothing or even a discarded gun. It began to rain soon after dark which turned heavy and they were all soaked having not been prepared for the weather, but it was essential they tried to find any evidence. All they had for light were their heavy oil lanterns. By the time dawn arrived they were muddy, tired and drenched through. They were all despondent as they had found nothing to help the investigation. The superintendent called a welcome halt for a rest and most trudged back towards the Knoll but an unfortunate few were left behind to stand guard over the Casa and all footpaths leading to it. A welcome breakfast and tea was provided by the Knoll staff in the kitchen.

5

TUESDAY

La Casa

As soon it was daylight on Tuesday morning the police numbering over thirty resumed their search of the woods. The police cordon of the immediate area remained and a special squad of police cyclists were patrolling the lanes and bridleways ensuring no one without a special permit was allowed to enter the area. Throughout the day curious locals lingered near the approaches to the Knoll discussing in whispers the murder and the numerous theories that were being rumoured. At one point a man was arrested on the estate raising the possibility they had found the culprit, but it was an unrelated incident. The situation was very tense.

A feeling of gloom descended over the village as no one could understand why Mrs Luard, who was so popular in the village, mainly because of her benevolence in the area, could have been targeted. Rumours abounded which became more ridiculous the longer time went by with no arrest or news. Just to stoke up the anxiety in the district one local newspaper stated:

> The murderer is still at large. This is not only the most sensational crime of the age, but one of the most mysterious, a lady of high social position, evidently without an enemy, taking her walks abroad daily in one of the most salubrious parts of the Garden of England. To be so foully murdered in broad daylight, just fifteen minutes after she left her husband to return home through a private path, and within shouting distance of other residents and the evil doer to get clean away without leaving the slightest clue behind, gives one the impression that the murderer is a villain of not only exceptional brutality, but cunning.

The district for a wide distance around the scene of the tragedy is covered with pine woods, and during the summer dense in undergrowth with a tangle of bramble and bracken except where intersected by footpaths. Although the rain had ceased the dense bracken was sodden and the pine and oak trees dripped from overhead to saturate the officers yet again. Many of them were not happy as they were convinced what they were doing was a waste of time believing the murderer was long gone. Even if there had ever been a chance of tracking foot marks, the heavy rain, which had fallen during the night, would have obliterated all traces and all the scouring, whether of woods or open country, was in vain. The only footprints found were leading from the Casa through a gate to the stables and some trodden down bracken was discovered leading to a hedge where it ended. They knew it would have been easy for the assailant to have made a clear getaway before any search was commenced with smaller railway stations like Kemsing and Wrotham close by and even Sevenoaks railway station not that far.

Detective Inspector Edwin Fowle arrived early Tuesday morning as promised with Detective Constables Thomas Gutteridge, Henry MacGovern and John Cockrell. 30-year-old Thomas Gutteridge was a close friend of Edwin's and his right-hand man and was soon to be his best man at his wedding. Taylor had also summoned another superintendent from neighbouring Malling division named Ford who helped supervise the manhunt.

When eventually the search of the woods and meadows was abandoned the investigation turned to the pond which the Casa overlooked and this was meticulously dragged, but nothing of interest was found. Then it was the turn of the well which was emptied but only years of general debris was discovered. Any fanciful thoughts of finding the murder weapon were all dashed.

Later in the morning Warde arrived and was greeted by Taylor and Edwin who led him to the scene advising him of the unsuccessful search that had taken place overnight. More out of despair than anything else, Warde ordered that the undergrowth must be cleared and the top soil turned over from around the Casa in the wild hope of obtaining any clue or piece of evidence. The main object of the search was to find the revolver which the murderer might for some bizarre reason have buried there or even the rings taken from the dead lady's fingers. Why the culprit would have buried his ill-gotten gains before he departed was not made clear as he would have been foolish indeed to have returned at a later date to retrieve them. Every spade full of soil was carefully sifted and examined, but the result was the same as the all the previious efforts. In the evening the digging operations were also abandoned.

After inspecting the murder scene Warde went to the Knoll to be greeted by his old friend the General and offered his condolences, promising him they would find the wretched fellow who had committed the heinous crime. He had previously ordered that his friend should not be formally interviewed until he was present, and when Taylor joined them, Edwin was dismissed to start interviewing all the witnesses. The General was still in a state of emotional collapse and unable to articulate enough to give them any tangible evidence but gave a statement. The Chief stayed with him accepting the offer of lunch. The staff who served them were in a miserable state with tears welling up every time they saw their distressed master. Sergeant was also despondent sensing that something was wrong and sat sullenly by his master or trotted round with his tail at half-mast.

After speaking to the General it was established which pieces of Caroline's jewellery had been stolen. These were a gold wedding ring, a gold diamond ring with an old setting, one large diamond ring surrounded by seven or eight small diamonds and a gold ring with the letters ISHI engraved in Asian script in blue enamel meaning husband plus a gold brooch. They immediately sent an alert by every means to police forces nationwide and particularly London asking for the descriptions to be relayed to jewellers and to report anyone trying to sell or pawn the items.

Warde was a worried man as he could see the case getting out of control unless it was solved quickly. He had already called in officers from all over the County to deal with the search and security of the area which was being already inundated with the press core and onlookers. This was seriously depleting resources in all the divisions, so he decided to take the unusual step of bringing in Scotland Yard even though his own detectives had only been on the case for a few hours. He discussed the idea with Taylor who finally acquiesced, but it was a somewhat strange decision as it was Warde who had created his own detective department to obviate the need of involving the Yard. Taylor knew that Edwin might be put out by the decision as a slight on his capabilities as he was nominally in charge of the investigation. Warde contacted the Yard and by late afternoon was on a train to London heading for the imposing red brick building overlooking the Thames at Westminster Bridge.

He had arranged a meeting with Sir Melville MacNaughton, another military gentleman who was head of the Criminal Investigation Department at the Yard. Warde knew him well as the two forces had close and regular contact due to their proximity and the fact that it was London criminals who regularly committed crimes in Kent before hightailing it back to the metropolis. At the Yard he met Chief Inspector Frank Froest, MacNaughton's deputy, a thick set and upright man who had a reputation for emphasising points in a level unemotional tone. The two entered MacNaughton's office with a view of the Thames and the tall grey-haired man, who was known for talking little but always to the point, stood to greet Warde.

Warde told the two men that he was a great friend of the Luards and had promised to do everything possible to find the murderer. The Yard men offered their condolences and were then informed of the facts so far surrounding the shooting particularly the General's statement and his high-profile position in the community being a J.P. They appreciated that the case would soon become a national sensation due to the victim's high status and the circumstances having all the aspects of a fictional whodunnit.

They promised to send help early next morning and following drinks, Warde returned to Kent.

After he left, the two senior officers had a consultation on who to send as they always used an officer of Chief Inspector rank and they had a few to choose from who covered different areas of London. It was a question of which one had the diplomacy and experience to assist in the case. They eventually narrowed it down to three: the well-known burly "debonair" Drew whose patch was the West End, Detective Kane who was known for his work on the Dublin Metropolitan police jewel mystery case in 1907 and Detective James Scott, a tall slim dour Scotsman with an exemplary arrest record. All three were viewed as shrewd, keen, and unemotional men, but they decided Scott was probably the best choice having the edge on being more tactful and able to work in parallel with possibly disgruntled local officers. He was told to make his way to Kent in the morning and to choose a Detective Sergeant to accompany him. He asked for Detective Sergeant Percy Savage, an experienced officer of seven years' service. In his autobiography, *Savage of Scotland Yard,* Percy Savage, who went on to be a superintendent, states rather presumptuously that he and Scott were "selected to take charge of the investigation and were most ably assisted by Supt. Taylor and other officers." It was such patronising statements that did not enamour provisional police towards the Yard. As it turned out the two Yard men did little to take the case forward and flitted between London and Kent spending the odd day here and there. Early next morning the duo set off by train to the perceived backwoods of Sevenoaks.

***

Meanwhile Edwin had been brought up to speed by Taylor about the General's interview, had thoroughly examined the murder scene and the body still lying in the bedroom, had immediately begun his enquiries, but first he took a few minutes to mull over what he had been told so far. During his twelve years as a detective he had learned that one of the first things a detective should do on gaining possession of all the facts is to deliberately analyse them and that is what he was doing now.

He always dreaded murder investigations as both the press and the public expected an almost immediate arrest and became critical and impatient when this did not happen. Murder was different from all other classes of crime because the search for a suspect is almost always a wide one especially when no motive is apparent, which it would appear on the surface was so in this case. The murderer could be anyone: the husband, a lunatic, tramp, footpad, relative, vindictive servant, anyone; and the motive robbery, revenge, jealousy, anything. Those not accustomed with investigating crime are unaware of the great part played by chance in aiding a detective. The press loved to rack up interest and spread rumour which frustrated and annoyed him. The amount of times he had read in the press that "the police have a clue." Clue as he well knew is an elastic word and may mean anything and usually means nothing.

So what are the initial obvious motives he said to himself. Both the victim and her husband were highly popular particularly as Mrs Luard was the "Lady Bountiful" of the neighbourhood. A local man had already said to him that, 'Mrs Luard was one of those who would always speak to a working man if she knew him. I remember last year when my arm was bad and I could not work, she met me twice and each time inquired how I was getting on and gave me something out of her purse as well. She was a very kind lady and always had a pleasant word for one.'

According to everyone he had spoken to so far, she was of a strong personality, intolerant of evil doing and not afraid of rebuking wrong doers no matter in what circumstances. It was common knowledge in the neighbourhood that Mrs Luard wore jewellery and carried money which would no doubt be judged in the eyes of impoverished and desperate vagrants as worth taking risks to steal.

Edwin realised that his investigations were going to be somewhat complicated by the fact that it was the "hopping" season when thousands of regular hoppers from London came down in special trains laid on for them to work in the hop fields. Although many farmers provided them with basic accommodation or camping grounds there was also an influx of vagrants, hawkers and villains who were rough sleepers in the woods hoping to either obtain a day's work here and there or fleece or steal from the others.

Although the law banned such activity some leniency was shown allowing them to camp for twenty-four hours on one spot before moving on but this was widely ignored as many set up camp in the middle of woods, and far from roads and tracks where they were not easily detected and remained for much longer periods. The large stretches of woodland around the Seal Chart estates with thick undergrowth of bracken and heather made it a favourite spot for numerous vagrants, viewed by landowners and villagers as a menace and nuisance and uncharitably referred to as pests. This situation was a regular disgruntlement and topic of intense conversation amongst locals and even more so because of the murder.

The General himself intimated in a letter to the *Sevenoaks Chronicle* on 8 September that it may have been one of these who killed his wife when he wrote:

> The public at large has been deeply disturbed by this awful crime, and I may have some rights to ask if the time has not arrived for clearing away from our roads, our lanes, and our woods, the many thousands of unemployed people, many of them in a desperate state, from want, that might give way to temptation and commit the worst of sins.

Edwin was well aware that the murderer could have been one of this "class" and that robbery was a distinct possibility but what were the chances of a vagrant carrying a revolver. Guns were readily available with many service pieces brought back from the numerous conflicts over the last decade circulating. He knew of many instances of armed rough sleepers and there were unfortunately many deranged persons roaming the countryside. But it would need a variety of chance events to have put Mrs Luard and an armed violent thief together at the Casa. More likely she arrived at the Casa to find someone intent on breaking in and had accosted him.

So what other common motives are there he perused, perhaps revenge of some sort? Local inhabitants all seem to agree she was a wonderful charitable lady with no enemies; so again doubtful. Jealousy maybe? Did she have a secret life of some kind or a secret lover? Mrs Luard was fifty-eight years old and married over twenty years which stretched the imagination somewhat to believe it was a question of jealousy or falling out with a lover. Anyway would you arrange a meet with a secret lover when you knew a guest was expected and arriving late was such a social faux pax in such circles. Suicide had been ruled out by the doctor. He decided that theories only muddied the waters and better to start with the basics. What am I left with he said to himself? The husband did it?

Edwin went off in search of Tom Gutteridge with the intention of beginning by confirming the husband's movements and alibi and finding out if the couple were as devoted as everybody believed.

***

Edwin and Tom began with interviewing the staff who were all in a distressed state having been devoted to their mistress. They spoke to them individually beginning with Harriet Huish the parlour-maid. She entered clutching a handkerchief and was asked to sit. Tom stood to the side taking notes.

'I know this is a difficult time. You must have known your mistress well I take it?'

'Yes, sir. I have been looking after her for six years. Right close we were,' replied Harriet beginning to whimper.

'Could you tell us the last time you saw Mrs Luard?'

'It was in the afternoon. The mistress called for me and told me she was going out to accompany the master for a walk, so I went upstairs with her to help her dress,' said the tearful Harriet.

'Can you remember what time this was?'

'At about twenty minutes past two.'

'And then what happened?'

'We came back downstairs, and she told me and cook that she was going to walk towards the golf links, but only part of the way and would be back as a visitor was coming to tea that afternoon.'

'Did she seem happy and her normal self?'

'Oh yes sir.'

'What time did they leave?'

'About two thirty, sir.'

'Were they a happy couple.'

'Very much so, devoted I would say.'

'And when they left they were on good terms?'

'Yes.'

Tom then fetched the other maid Jane Pugmore, who was similarly suffering from the loss of her mistress.

'How long have you been in service here.'

'Six years, sir.'

'So you know your master and mistress very well.'

'Yes sir, always very kind to us servants.'

'Did they get on well?'

'Of course, they lived on the very happiest terms.'

The staff all confirmed that their master kept three revolvers or pistols in the house in various strategic places lest burglars entered the house. One was in his study, another in the library, and bizarrely according to Jane, one in the bathroom cupboard covered up with some cloths presumably in case he happened to be in the bath or on the commode when the house was invaded. He later admitted that none were ever actually loaded.

Once they had spoken to the household staff they made their way over to the Frankfield farmhouse and spoke to the staff there. Edwin and Tom searched out Herbert Hamilton Harding, Mr Wilkinson's butler and he conveyed the events of that afternoon in which he was involved when he accompanied the General back to the Casa at about 5.30pm. Then it was the turn of Daniel Kettle, Mr Wilkinson's aged gardener who was asked whether he had heard any shots that afternoon.

'Not as many as we usually get, sir.'

'But did you hear any that afternoon?'

'I do remember hearing maybe three as I was coming down the drive at about quarter past three.'

'Do you remember if they were fired all at the same time?'

'Now you mention it there was a pause between the first and the other two, but my hearing ain't that good. I'm 73 years old you know.'

'How far were you from the Casa?'

'About a quarter a mile or so I'd say.'

'Were they coming from that direction?'

'Difficult to tell. My hearing is not so good,' he repeated, 'I just thought it was a farmer nearby shooting squirrels. He often does.'

The two officers then went to Wickham's cottage and spoke to Annie Wickham, the coachman's wife who also stated she heard the shots.

'Did you see the General that afternoon?' asked Edwin.

'It was a strange afternoon Inspector, unusually quiet, and even the Jays had been silent. I was sitting outside with my daughter Edith knitting and I remember thinking it was one of those times when you got a little shiver, like something was going to happen. I remember at about quarter past three I heard three shots coming from the direction of the summerhouse. The first one seemed to have a very strange sound and as if it had struck something. We're used to the sounds of shooting as its good sporting country. And when I heard the next two shots I turned to Edith who was sitting beside me and said, 'they really mean to kill whatever they're shooting at.'

'And the General?'

'Oh yes, that was later, awful it was. Never seen him in such a state, hardly recognised him. About half past five he came rushing into the yard almost collapsing at our feet, coming from the direction of the summer house. I asks him what on earth is the matter and out of breath like, he said, "I have some very great trouble," which was obvious to see. He then asked where my husband was, and I told him he was at the stables. I could see he was upset and I asked him if we could help but he made no reply but staggered off to find my husband leaving us wondering.'

The Reverend Arthur Benjaman Cotton who lived at Shepbourne Grange came forward with information. He was a typical middle-aged country clergyman, bespectacled with a balding grey hair and beard. On the afternoon of the murder he was out and about in the wood close to the murder scene with some ladies who were taking photographs. While he was standing with them he saw the General approaching, with Sergeant at about ten past four. He noticed he was carrying some golf clubs and as he came up to him they exchanged greetings and Cotton asked where he was going. The General told him he was off home so he offered him a lift in his car, but he declined saying he needed the exercise but Cotton then offered to drop his clubs at the Knoll. This the General accepted and he set off again walking towards Ightham. When the Reverend was driving home he saw the rather hot General walking along the road at about twenty past four and this time he accepted a lift and got out at the gate of his drive. This was about twenty minutes later at four thirty.

Thomas Durrant, the manager of the local Blythe's Brewery was also out and about that afternoon and Edwin caught up with him for an interview.

'Did you see the General?'

'Yes.'

'Whereabouts was this.'

'I was at the top of Hall Hill, and I saw him going through the gateway at the top of Hall Farm by the fir trees at about two thirty.'

'Did he have anyone and anything with him?'

'Only his old Irish terrier, Sergeant. I had my little fox terrier with me, and he ran away with Sergeant. They had a right scamper. Lovely dog that.'

'Did you speak to him?'

'No, but he smiled and nodded.'

'Did he seem alright?'

'As far as I noticed. He seemed in a hurry, walking fast like.'

A labourer named Ernest King who lived at Hall Cottage, Godden Green also came forward.

'Did you see the General that afternoon,'

'I did sir.'

'Where was he going?'

'Heading in the direction of the Golf links.'

'What time was this?'

'It was between three twenty-five and half past I reckon.'

'You seem definite about the time, how's that?'

'I am, sir. You see, I looked at my watch about a minute before he appeared to check if it was near home time.'

'Did you see him again'?'

'Yes, about ten minutes later.'

'Did he seem in a hurry or upset in any way?'

'Not that I can recollect. He was carrying some golf clubs though.'

'How far were you from the links?'

'I'd say about two hundred yards from the golf house.'

Edwin and Tom then made their way to the Godden Green post office to speak to Harry Kent the sub-postmaster who was also the chairman of the golf club. He kept chickens in the corner of the grounds and was walking across the links heading to feed them when he came across the General.

'I understand you saw the General while walking across the course?'

'Yes I met him on the eighth hole.'

'Did he have golf clubs with him?'

'He did,'

'What time was this would you say?'

'Must have been about half past three.'

Having spoken to most of the witnesses they were aware of Edwin called a meeting of his detectives to run through what they had gleaned in regard to the General's movements that afternoon and whether he had a sound alibi and if not what were the other possibilities.

'We know that Mrs Luard had several favourite haunts in the woods which she liked to walk to, often alone, but these walks were not necessarily regular. This would make it difficult for an assailant to be lying in wait for her as it was not a daily occurrence. More likely it was a chance event. During this season of the year, when hop picking is starting, the whole countryside is infested with persons of the roughest type and all sorts of queer characters. Possibly among this motley crowd an armed criminal might have lurked possibly hiding in the woods with the object to plunder from one of the isolated houses round and about. He may even have been sizing up the summerhouse and decided Mrs Luard was easy prey. This is going to be a difficult investigation, but it might be possible to rule out our prime suspect, the General. Here's the timetable of his movements as far as I can gather:'

2.30pm The General and his wife left the house to visit Goddon Green Golf Links. They walked together through the Fish Pond wood, passing half a mile from home until they got to the wicket gate.

3pm about, Mrs Luard left the General at the wicket gate to retrace her steps to her house where a lady guest was expected for tea at 4.30pm. The General continued in the opposite direction on his walk to the golf links.

3.15pm shots were heard by Daniel Kettle, the gardener, and Mrs Wickham, the coachman's wife, of Frankfield Farm. Strange though that Fred Wickham heard nothing as he was in the same area.

At 3:20 pm, Mr. Thomas Durrent, the brewery manager, saw the General on Hall Hill near Hall Farm. This spot would be a ten-to-fifteen-minute walk from the Casa.

3.25pm Richard King a labourer saw the General some four hundred yards away from where Durrant saw him.

3.30pm Harry Kent, the sub postmaster at Goddon Green saw the General at the golf links, less than two miles from where shots were heard only a quarter an hour before. The General having obtained his clubs started for home by a different route along the main road, Stone Street.

4.10pm The Reverend Arthur Benjamin Cotton saw the General in the woods about half a mile from the scene of the murder carrying his golf clubs and accompanied by his dog. Mr Cotton offered to give him a lift in his motor car, but he declined at first and then put the clubs in the car. Mr Cotton, who was driving very slowly came across him again further along and this time accepted a ride and was driven to the Knoll which was reached at 4.30pm.

4.30pm. The General meets Mrs Stewart, the lady who was expected to tea waiting for him at his house. Between that hour and 5pm, the General and Mrs Stewart had tea then left to seek his wife.

5.15pm. Mrs Stewart left the General to continue alone to find his wife. Finding his murdered wife at the Casa he goes in search of help.

5.30pm. The General reaches Mrs Wickham's house seeking help.

5.35pm He reaches Frankfield farmhouse where Mr Butler accompanies him to the scene of the tragedy.

So there we have it in a nutshell, and it would appear that the General is in the clear, at the moment anyway, but we need to do more digging and if he is not the murderer we need to find out who is pronto.'

***

The post mortem was conducted on Tuesday evening by Dr. Mansfield and Dr E Walker of Ightham. All the senior officers including Edwin were present to listen to the findings. Both physicians agreed that the bullet wounds could not have been self-inflicted.

The doctors examined her arms but there were no signs of bruising or injury, but there was bruising on her right cheek and chin and some to her nose. There was a bullet hole behind her right ear with blackening around it about two inches in diameter and a similar mark around the bullet hole over the left cheek. There was no trace of powder burns in the eye suggesting that the eye must have been closed when the shots were fired. They found the remains of a bullet in a space of about two and a half inches diameter in front of the parietal eminence where blood had collected and within it was the shattered fragments of a bullet. When they removed the brain, they found a second intact but flattened bullet. Later the fragments of the first bullet were carefully removed, put together and weighed and the weight exactly corresponded with the other bullet which was found intact. Although witnesses were adamant that they heard three shots that afternoon there was no sign of a third bullet in the body. The bullet and fragments were taken to a London gun expert for analysis.

Dr Mansfield's theory was that she had been hit from behind while the heart was beating strongly causing much bleeding and fell face down on the ground causing her to vomit. She was then shot at close range behind the right ear and when this did not kill her, as it hit the hardest part of the skull, another shot was fired. Dr. Walker agreed with his colleague on the shooting sequence but was adamant that she wasn't hit over the head by an assailant but shot first causing her to hit her head on a pillar as she fell. There was no indication of any other assault. They pronounced cause of death as bullet wounds to the head.

6

THE INQUEST

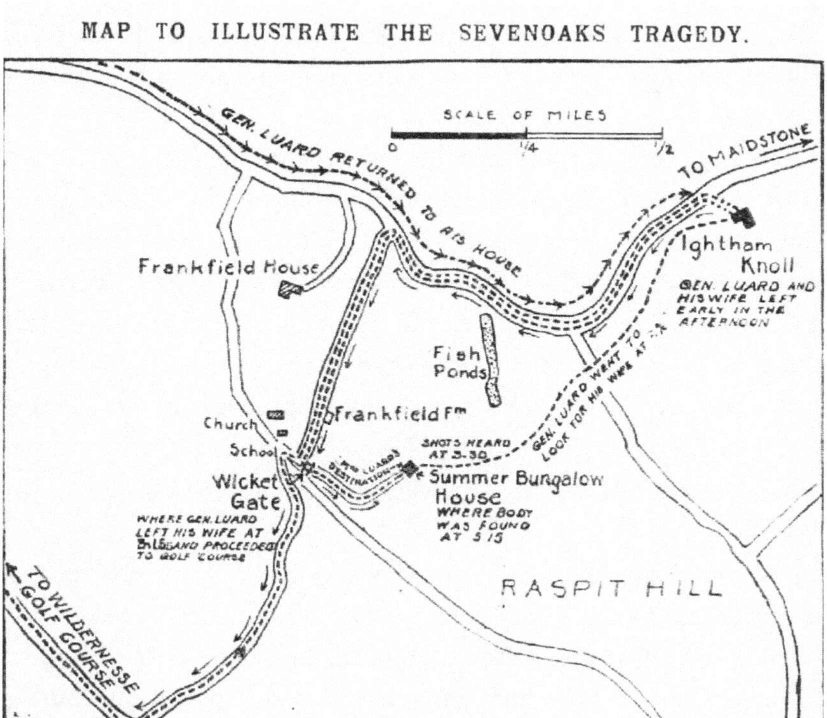

Sketch map of the fateful walk

When Edwin arrived early on Tuesday morning for the inquest the constables had difficulty gaining him access to the drive up to the house as he had to run the gauntlet of droves of press reporters and onlookers. It was the same in the following days whenever he departed or returned from following up leads or interviewing possible suspects or witnesses. On one side there were normally about a dozen photographers with all their paraphernalia and on the other another thirty odd journalists in small groups discussing the case and information they had gathered. Two constables stationed there had to part the crowd to let every visitor through. This did not enamour them any further in Edwin's opinion.

He also did not think they showed the police the respect they were due or appreciated the difficulties they had in investigating the case. Although it was 1908 and motor cars were becoming more common, the Kent force did not possess one. They were still stuck in the Victorian era and did not even have that many bicycles to share round. Only superintendents had the luxury of a one-horse trap and driver. This fact was well-known to the pressmen, and every time Taylor with his driver passed through they somewhat derisively played on this by heckling and referring to it as the "Super's" trap.

As the days passed the press became more of an obstruction to the investigation. They were well organised, almost like a military operation and had set up their headquarters at the Rose and Crown Hotel in Wrotham high street, just a five-minute drive from the action. They were using the tavern rather like the famous Cheshire Cheese pub in London's Fleet Street where reporters historically collected to swap the day's news and anecdotes. The London agencies and newspaper reporters had a large budget from their editors and rented cars from local owners or garages which was good income for them. The journalists had also forged profitable relationships with certain officials and locals and received tip offs about upcoming interviews of possible witnesses or culprits. In this way the press sometimes arrived before the police and were found to be interviewing people before they had a chance. Failing this the journalists would wait in their cars for any sign of police movement and then follow the officers who in their traps or carriages could not outrun them.

It became so bad that ultimately Taylor was forced to resort to subterfuge. It then became a cat and mouse scenario with the police having to formulate military style plans to match the press in order to work unhindered. On one occasion there was a humorous "dodging" incident when Taylor and Edwin needed to travel to the Tonbridge Pembury Union workhouse to interview a man who could not give an account of himself or his movements at the time of the murder. It was an important lead, and they did not want the press interfering, so they hatched a plan. They got into the superintendent's trap driven by Constable Hill, his driver, and gently trotted down the road as if they were out on a pleasant ride in the countryside. The journalists watched with interest dithering as to whether it was worth following them but not concerned as they knew they could easily catch them up. The constable turned into a field, and they swapped into another carriage which was waiting for them and headed off at a fast trot. The press eventually became suspicious and chased after them in their cars but soon came across the returning trap empty of its passengers being driven back by Constable Hill and blocking the narrow track. Although he was intensely questioned and encouraged he refused to divulge their whereabouts.

The *Kentish Chronicle* reported that it had become "a case of diamond-cuts-diamond," meaning evenly matched in wits or cunning and stated that "in sunshine and in rain have the police pursued their investigations and in sunshine and in rain have the journalists pursued the police."

Edwin for one wanted the lot of them arrested and said the whole investigation was becoming a three-ring circus. What with the unnecessary Scotland Yard involvement, the Chief Constable taking over the case against normal protocol and press interference he had no wonder they were not getting anywhere.

Eventually this subterfuge was too great an irritant and Warde decided to invest in hiring a car and not just any old car. He went to H.E. Hall & Company of Tonbridge and took delivery of a 18hp Germain motor car, which according to advertisements had a "speed only matched by the nerve of the driver and is well suited for negotiating hilly country roads." Mr Hall was quick to promote his car by writing a letter to the newspapers extolling its virtues stating he had "placed it at the disposal of the police" and it was being driven by his son. He stated that "we are quite safe in saying that during the days and nights since the crime the authorities have been enabled to cover ground, which, with other conveyance than a fast motor car, would have taken weeks." Obviously the salesman saw the Chief Constable coming.

The choice of car though was unfortunate, or the colour anyway, as it was bright yellow and could not have been more conspicuous. The press loved it as it gave more scope to mock the police by nicknaming it "The Butterfly" because it had a large yellow butterfly painted on the radiator. It also gave Edwin the opportunity to state that he felt like a clown sitting in it and the investigation had become even more of a circus. Luckily for him he did not get much chance of riding in it as unsurprisingly it was mostly requisitioned by Warde and Chief Inspector Scott. It became famous at the time and much publicised, but it was of little value as the press just drove quicker turning the lanes into something like the newly opened Brooklands racetrack.

When Foster arrived outside Ightham Knoll on the morning of the inquest even he was amazed at how many journalists had already assembled. Although he was well known to most of the local police officers he could not penetrate the cordon which had sealed off every approach to the Casa and the Knoll and was forced to stand outside the gate with all the others. His usual friendly repartee and pleading with the local constables had fallen on deaf ears and they were not willing to do him any favours. As he wandered amongst his colleagues he noticed all the London newspapers were there, some having two or three representatives, and the major news agencies were also present. Messengers were eagerly hovering in readiness to take batches of copy to the nearest telephone or telegraph office and motor cars and horse and traps were parked up for them to use. The main topic of conversation was how to gain access to the inquest.

At about midday they watched Supt. Taylor and Detective Scott hastily drive from the scene which caused rumours of possible clues or arrests. A couple of minutes later they returned and were seen to alight and talk earnestly with Edwin and Supt. Ford outside the house. Then Sergeant Paramour could be seen joining the discussion group causing more speculation. They were in fact discussing what was to be done about the press contingent as they realised they could have a riot on their hands if they barred access.

Although the inquest was timed for 3.15pm a crowd had already gathered by noon at the entrance gate to the drive. They were descending on the scene using any kind of transport they could muster and their traps, carriages, motor cycles, bicycles and motor cars were causing jams on the narrow lanes for far around. Those without transport were arriving at Borough Green train station and walking the mile to the scene. All were discussing the murder and the possibilities of an arrest. Every official car containing police officers or other officials were gawped at and their occupants inspected. When the Chief Constable arrived at 2pm with his deputy Captain Lafone the crowd became more difficult to push back and scuffles broke out to take photographs and shout questions. It was a struggle to gain entry through the throng and they remained sternly silent to all the heckling.

As the start time for the inquest approached the patience of the press began to recede and their mood became irritable when a rumour spread that only three pressman were to be admitted. At the same time as those in the house were discussing the problem the reporters were also having a conference as to who should be the chosen ones if it came to that. This was interrupted when Taylor and Sergeant Paramour appeared at the bend in the driveway and a message was sent to the Constables on the gate. One of them shouted for silence and the journalists jostled forward. The constable shouted in a loud voice, 'Would Mr Foster McAdam of the Sevenoaks Chronicle please step forward.' Foster had been chosen by the police as a go between as he represented the major local newspaper for the district and was known to them.

Foster couldn't believe his luck and immediately stepped forward and hurried through the gate pushed ajar by the constable while his colleagues looked on malevolently. It was his coverage in the local *Sevenoaks Chronicle* that had brought them all here when he had broken the story. He joined the superintendent who explained that only six men could be entertained and that he had the unenviable task of choosing the others amongst his colleagues more fairly than he could hope to. Foster called a reporter friend named Kendall to join him and they went into a huddle to start going through names first suggesting drawing straws, but Taylor dismissed this as it would be too time consuming and complicated.

Their colleagues expecting to be let through had taken advantage of the confused constables by filtering through the gate, but Foster stopped them in their tracks and explained the situation. There was an angry uproar of voices for a while, but Foster calmed them and with his colleague by his side stared back at the throng of expectant faces and whispered to each other for a few minutes and then shouted the names of Mr Sandeman of the Press Association, the Daily Mail journalist, the Central News representative and one other local colleague. The agreement was that they all would share their copy with the unlucky ones to meet the deadline for the late evening papers which would enable all the London and provincial newspapers to report "one of the most sensational murders of the age." Although those left out of witnessing it first-hand remained disgruntled, and some still very angry at what they believed to be an attack on the freedom of the press they accepted the situation. A bit of a scrum then commenced when the unlucky ones had to be removed from the drive back behind the gate, but the press siege remained.

The ire of the press continued and the *Globe* newspaper on the front page of their 27 August issue vented its thoughts, making their feelings plain:

> We All, as a rule, are very loathe to criticise the arrangements made by the authorities for the accommodation of the press on important occasions. Usually there is no ground for complaints. Those who have the control of these matters recognise responsibilities which are laid upon the shoulders of the reporter. It is therefore with great regret that we are compelled to protest against the utter and need-

> less inaccuracy of the arrangements made at Ightham. The coroner can hardly be unaware that the murder of Mrs Luard has excited the deepest interest throughout the length and breadth of the country. And that in view of the mystery surrounding the crime, it is of the greatest importance that as many members of the public as possible should have an opportunity of reading reports of the inquest. The problem before the police is one of the utmost difficulty, and it might very well be that one of the public knowing perhaps some special feature of the district or personally aware of some persons suspicious movements might by comparing various reports supply them with a valuable clue. In Ightham village there is a hall in which ample accommodation for the press could be provided. And yet, in spite of this, the inquest was held in General Luard's private house, where, of course, nothing of the kind was possible. As a result, only four [six actually] out of nearly 40 reporters were admitted. Any excluded were roughly hustled away by the police as if they were mere sightseers instead of professional men charged with a great responsibility and anxious only to do their duty. Those authorities who show so little consideration for the press, can hardly expect its assistance when, as happens again and again, they are compelled to appeal for it.

Meanwhile everyone connected with the inquest were taking their seats and watched in surprise as the six hot and flustered pressmen rushed to grab their seats. Edwin was still slumped in his allocated seat and being a dog lover had been watching Sergeant wander from room to room not quite understanding who all these people were who had invaded his house and inspecting all the upended furniture. More importantly he seemed to be searching for his missing mistress amongst all the chaos. He was receiving the odd stroke and whispered greeting including from Edwin who felt sorry for him. That morning Sergeant had accompanied the General as he walked around the grounds of the house out of the view of all the onlookers looking exhausted and in ill health.

When the inquest finally got under way Paramour stood at the dining room door and called the first witness, the General. He looked frail and beaten as he tried to keep his bearing as he entered into the room supported by a friend. He literally sank into the witness chair with Sergeant beside him, leaning down to give him a sad smile as though appreciating his fidelity and fondly patted him. He stated that his wife was fifty-eight years of age, and they had lived together happily for twenty years at Ightham Knoll.

The coroner asked, 'Was she in good health on Monday last?'

'Yes,' whispered the General.

'Can you describe your movements that afternoon?'

'I left the house with my wife a little before 2.30pm. It was my intention to collect some clubs from the Godden Green Golf links and she said she would accompany me part of the way and we went through Fish Pond Wood.'

'How far did your wife accompany you?'

'We walked as far as some gates at the top of the narrow lane, which leads upwards from Mr Wilkinson's coachman's house. We parted near Saint Lawrence's School.'

'She left you and you continued your journey?'

'Yes.'

'She expected someone to tea, is that right?'

'That's right.'

'So she turned? Did you notice which way she went home?'

'Yes. For a few yards you can see the path from the gates, and after that you lose sight of it.'

'After that you went and got your clubs and came back. Is that right?'

'Correct. I went on to the golf links, got my clubs and arrived home at four thirty.'

'Your visitor, Mrs Stewart, had already arrived when you reached home?'

'Yes. We had tea.'

'But your wife didn't arrive?'

'No.'

'So what did you do then?'

'I told Mrs Stewart I would go and look for her up the path to the summerhouse and she came with me.'

'Did you both reach the summerhouse?'

'No. Mrs Stewart turned round at five thirty. I know it was that time because she told me she had to meet somebody off the train, and she looked at her watch.'

'You went on the path you knew your wife was coming back on?'

'Yes, exactly the same path we had taken previously.'

'You did not see her on the track, so you went to the summer house, is that right?'

'Yes, I had expected to meet her on the track but did not.'

'Did you see anybody else on the track?'

'Not from the time I left the high road or in the woods.'

He was then asked if he saw his wife when he got to the summerhouse and he shuddered at his recollection of what he had seen.

'Yes, I have written it all down of what I saw.' Then pausing, as if seeking to avoid the repetition of the painful narrative he continued in a plaintive tone, 'Please read it and I will say if it is correct, will you?'

The coroner had before him several sheets of foolscap paper containing the General's own statement of the discovery. He took him through this as briefly as possible.

'You saw your wife lying on the floor of the veranda, is that right?'

'Yes.'

'You thought she was in a fainting fit?'

'I did.'

'On going closer, you saw the blood on the floor?'

'Yes, I did.'

'You thought she had burst a blood vessel?'

'I thought that possibly she had.'

'And ongoing still closer you saw that her head and face was covered with blood?'

'Yes, not so much her face as her head.'

'She was lying partly on her face. Is that correct?'

'Yes.'

'You took one of her hands and tried to feel her pulse. The hand was cold?'

'Quite.'

'You then concluded she was dead?'

The General, in a scarcely audible whisper, replied yes, at the same time nodding his head in affirmation.

' And you saw one of her gloves was turned inside out?'

'Yes, as though it had been wrenched off her.'

'Observing her hand, did you notice that the rings were missing?'

'I did?'

'Which hand would that be?'

'She wore her rings on the left hand.'

'Did you notice if the fingers were scarred or bruised?'

'No, I did not. They did not seem to be. I did not notice anything.'

'Did you notice whether your wife had her rings on when she left home that day?'

'I know she had. She always wore them, except when she washed her hands.'

'Was there anything particular about them?'

'One ring must have been about 100 years old. It was given to her by her mother. It had an old design of mounting.'

'Do you know whether she had any money when you left her?'

'I cannot say.'

'Have you or your wife ever had a revolver in your possession? '

'I have several revolvers in the house, but my wife never had one.'

'Would she be able to get possession of them or did you keep them locked up?'

'There is one in the library in its case, and two others in other rooms.'

'Did you make an examination of the bungalow to see if anyone had been about?'

'No.'

'As far as you know was there anyone who was likely to do anything of this sort to her? Was she unfriendly with anybody or had she any enemies?'

'No one at all. It's unthinkable.'

'Since the murder have you missed a revolver?'

'Oh no. The revolvers are in the same place as usual.'

'Do you mind fetching them.'

The General struggled up and disappeared from the room returning a while later with the revolvers and showed them.'

A juryman then surprised the General by asking, 'has the General any relation in an asylum who might have a grudge against Mrs Luard?'

'Certainly not.'

The two doctors were then called and explained the findings of the post mortem explaining that there was a bullet hole one inch behind her right ear with blackening round it. On closer examination he found another small bullet hole on her left temple half an inch behind the corner of the eye with blood that had seeped from it. He placed a pencil in the holes to determine the direction taken by the bullets. The hole behind her ear passed slightly forward and a little upward and was one inch deep. On the left side the pencil projected slightly upwards and backwards and was three inches deep. The only other signs of injury he could find were three small abrasions on the fingers of her left hand.

After this Dr Mansfield was asked whether he thought she could have shot herself. He replied it was virtually impossible as she would have needed two guns, one in each hand, and being right-handed, it would have required her to turn her head to the left for the first shot and then to the right for the second simultaneously. As the damage to the system was caused by the first shot it made it impossible for her to have made the second shot. Dr. Walker corroborated the details of Dr Mansfield but thought that the wounds on the head was not inflicted by physical violence but was result of the fall.

Then the house staff, those at the Frankfield estate and others who had witnessed the General's movements gave their evidence and the inquest was adjourned to Wednesday, 9 September awaiting more evidence from a gun expert who had been tasked with evaluating the crime scene and examining the bullets.

The expert was Edwin John Churchill, a gun and rifle manufacturer of 8 Agar St, London, who had been sent the bullets on the 27 August. He then came down from London with Scott to view the crime scene and perform a reconstruction of the murder. Edwin, along Warde, Major Lefone, Supt Taylor and Supt Ford all accompanied them to the Casa. All the men had taken another general survey of the bungalow and the path with a lot of rubbing of chins. They then walked to the wicket gate two hundred yards away where the couple had parted and then back to the veranda. Scott walked along the line Caroline would have done onto the veranda to the spot where she was shot. He laid down in the position she was found. They then discussed where the shooter may have been hiding to approach her. Mr Churchill re-enacted how the revolver was used to shoot her and the distance the gun would have been fired from her head. He then crawled round the veranda minutely examining the floor and walls in search of the elusive third bullet. After an hour he sat up with a broad grin and sensationally exclaimed, 'I have found the third bullet!' All the others rushed over and he pointed to a bullet hole. Although everyone was elated none of this proved of any value.

***

On Wednesday 9 September at 3pm. the second inquest hearing was held in the large assembly room at the old timbered George and Dragon Hotel on Fen Pond Road in the centre of Ightham village. Because of the publicity surrounding the case people had driven in their motor cars or arrived by train from as far afield as London to be there. A crowd numbering in the hundreds stood in the narrow street outside the hotel. There was more space this time to accommodate the press who literally crammed themselves into the room on a long table. Those that could not find space at the table stood inside and those outside were kept informed of what was happening. The room had very bad acoustics raising complaints from the correspondents that they could not hear the witnesses. All the witnesses from the earlier inquest were recalled and repeated their evidence. The General was not pleased at having to attend again but his attendance had been insisted upon to answer new questions and the journalists were intrigued to know what they were.

The haggard General walked with firm steps to the chair and sat down and answered questions in a quiet sorrowful voice.

'First of all, is there any incidents in the lives of the deceased or yourself which, in your opinion, would cause any person to entertain feelings of revenge or jealousy towards either of you?' asked the coroner.

'No, I don't think so.'

'Did your wife or did you at any time receive a letter from anyone which would lead you to suppose that any bad feelings were entertained towards her?'

'No. I don't remember any letter from anyone.'

'Did your wife recently before her death receive a letter making an appointment with her?'

'Yes, invitations of all sorts and kinds.'

'I mean any obscure appointment?'

'Oh no, she would certainly have told me if she had.'

The few more questions that had been anticipated turned into a long list. He went on to ask whether his wife had been in fear of anyone, knew anyone exhibiting symptoms of homicidal mania, and whether she suffered from any history of insanity. Then he quizzed the General on his guns.

'I understand you have several revolvers in your possession. Are you in the habit of carrying one?'

'Certainly not.'

'Had you one with you on the day of the murder?'

'Of course not.'

A juryman then asked if he had Sergeant with him and if the dog would have barked if anyone suspicious was about and the General replied 'Certainly.'

Edwin John Churchill, gun expert, was then called and explained that after examining and weighing them he confirmed they were of .320 short bore, a common cartridge in several guns. He was asked:

'In the case of the bullet wound behind the right ear, how close was the gun fired?

'By the blackening round the wound caused by the bullet, I should suggest it was quite close or about an inch behind the right ear,' replied Churchill.

'In regard to the other bullet wound, what would be the position?

'Well I should say that might have been two or three inches.'

'Have you been shown the revolvers belonging to the General?'

'I have not seen the revolvers at present.'

The coroner asked for the revolvers from Ightham Knoll to be handed to Mr Churchill, who, after examining them, said one was a Webley which fired .450 or .455 cartridges and the other a Colt double action.'

'So it would be impossible for the bullets found in the head of the dead body to have been fired from either of these?'

'Impossible.'

The third gun was then produced and Mr Churchill was asked to inspect this weapon. He pulled the trigger and remarked that it was quite an old-fashioned toy, used for practise at a very close distance and made by Broussard's.

'Might it be possible to kill anyone with a weapon of that kind?'

'No. Quite impossible.'

'After examining the cartridges at your workshop you suggested it would be a good idea if you made a close inspection at the summerhouse?'

'I did.'

He then explained that he had gone to Sevenoaks for that purpose in the company of Superintendent Taylor and Inspector Scott and examined the summerhouse floor and the fences around. He told the court he had found a great many bullet holes on the upright posts supporting the veranda and they were much smaller holes than made by the .320 bore. They were conical .22's and obviously caused by a gentlemen at some stage having been practising with an air gun. They were quite different from the bullets found in the deceased head. He then quite sensationally revealed that on examining the veranda floor he had found a bullet hole filled with particles of lead and blood at the spot where Mrs Luard's head had rested after she was turned over which he believed was the second or third shot fired in quick succession. The first shot would have knocked the lady down.

Mr Churchill was then asked if he could account why two witnesses had remarked that the first shot had a deadened sound compared with the subsequent shots.

'Yes sir, I can. A shot fired close to an object such as a human body would sound more like a thud. The gases would not have a chance to expand, and the thin grains of powder with which the cartridge is loaded would make a spread of about an inch and a half. The dull sound would be accounted for by the closeness of which the weapon was held.'

'Can you give us any idea as to what distance a glancing shot would bound to?'

'It might split up into smithereens.'

'It would not be found intact.'

'No. I spoke to Mrs Wickham and her statement confirmed my ideas that the second and third shots would have been much louder than the first.'

'Could you suggest at all whether these bullet wounds were self-inflicted?'

'They could not have been. Even if it were possible for the lady to inflict the first of them, it would have been an utter impossibility for her to inflict the second shot.'

'Have you any doubt that there were three shots fired?'

'No doubt whatsoever.'

'Is the size of the revolver used by the murderer a common size?'

'Yes, an old army type.'

Mr Churchill then took a revolver from his pocket and detached the chamber and brandished it to show the size of the bullet it would carry.

'The bullets in Mrs Luard's body would have been fired from such a revolver.'

Superintendent Taylor made a joke as the expert drew the revolver from his pocket and with a smile asked if it was a loaded and Mr Churchill smiled back and said it was not. He was then asked whether it was easy to acquire such a gun.

'Yes. You can get one for a pound upwards and there are so many foreign ones easily available.'

The coroner had a brief conversation with Warde and addressed the jury, 'The Chief Constable hopes that in the near future someone will be found who is responsible for this crime,' and then proceeded to adjourn the case yet again until the 23 September to many quiet groans. This somewhat bewildered everyone present as at the end of all the evidence there was absolutely nothing which even remotely pointed to the identity of the murderer.

On the 23 September the last inquest was a quick affair with little to discuss as the police, as everyone had expected, had no new evidence so Thomas Buss ended the inquest and on the jury's verdict he announced the decision of murder by persons unknown.

***

On the afternoon of Friday 28 August the weather was awful with torrential rain showers and very short intervals of sunshine. It was the day of Mrs Luard's funeral and the weather did not help the mood of all those attending. Over one hundred mourners were gathering outside the church under umbrellas or sheltering in their carriages and motor cars awaiting the 3.15pm start, each clutching a wreath which when laid on the grave completely covered it and a large area beyond. Each had a poignant message of sympathy particularly from family members. Her sister wrote "With the love of a lifetime" and another "With love and in affectionate remembrance Dear Aunty Daisy." And even more touchingly showing the regard the staff had for her, "From her sorrowing servants with sincere regret, Minnie, Huish and James."

There was little conversation amongst the solemn groups, many of them still coming to terms with the awful loss and circumstances of her death. Many realised the unfortunate coincidence of the timing of the funeral which was exactly the time when the fatal shots were supposed to have been fired that killed her and was also the time to the very minute at which the inquest was convened. Another sad feature was that Caroline's birthday fell on the day before the funeral. This made it even harder for many to bear.

The weather did not stop some local people from neighbouring villages congregating to silently watch the long procession pass through Ightham on the half mile journey to the church. Every household had drawn their blinds as was tradition and most of the little shops had closed. Her body was carried in an open hearse followed by the General and some other close family including his brother-in-law Mr Tom Hartley, in a waggonette loaned by Charles's closest neighbour Baronet Sir William Boord. Behind them were another dozen closed carriages which wound their way up the steep lane to the ancient St Peter's parish church. As the hearse approached, the men in the crowd uncovered their heads despite the heavy downpour, while it was noted that many of the ladies were visibly affected. When they arrived the muffled bells could be heard and they were greeted outside by about a hundred silent people drenched to the skin with a similar number inside the small church. All the men were dressed in dark coats and top hats and the women in dark cloaks, hats and veils. It was quite a sight for the onlookers. On arrival Mr Hartley had to support the General as he stepped from the carriage and through the graveyard into the church.

The coffin was of polished oak with brass furnishings and the plate had the following inscription: "Caroline Luard, Wife of Major General C.E. Luard, born 27th of August 1849, Died 24th of August 1908. Once the coffin had been placed inside, literally hidden beneath a hundred floral tributes, the various morning coaches gradually emptied the distinguished mourners. It was an impressive and huge gathering, a veritable Who's Who of Kent society and landed gentry, clergy and military from all over the country. The Luard's staff were present and even the seventeen members of the inquest jury. As the procession passed through to the church, all the police officers on duty in the lane stood at the salute as did Edwin, Superintendent Taylor, Superintendent Ford,

Chief Detective Scott and the Chief Constable who were lined up at the entrance.

The church was packed from end to end. The General was conducted to his seat in the front pew on the left-hand side. The relatives and the servants of the household sat in the pews on the other side of the aisle. The Rev. Winnifrith, Rector of Ightham, with Rev. Hill Scott, Vicar of Seal Chart and Reverend J Guise, Rector of Addington officiated. The service began with chanting by the choir of Psalm 39 and then Rev. Guise spoke:

> Five years ago, I was privileged to say a few words in this church on the occasion of a memorial service for our dear friend's son, Lieutenant Eric Luard. Today we have come to bury the mother of that soldier. It was at her request that I spoke a few words on the first occasion, and I'm asked to do the same at her funeral. The death we mourn today is due not to the severity of nature, but to the cruelty of man, but we do not come within these sacred walls to hear about the atrocious crime. It is difficult to comprehend how one so sweet natured, so gentle, so sympathetic to her neighbours, should be taken away in such a brutal manner. It is a terrible thing that, in these days of civilisation and enlightenment such a thing could be possible. Mrs Luard made herself loved and respected, and on every occasion she did what lay in her power in the way of sympathy and charity.

At the end of the service the funeral procession was reformed and the coffin slowly passed out of the church into the graveyard. Everyone then made their way up the hill to the churchyard, and with so many attending they were forced to find what room they could amongst the grave stones and on either side of the path in the north corner where the Luard family plot was situated. The rain refused to stop beating down and all that could be seen was a mass of black umbrellas being held stoically in the full force of the storm.

The General stood at the graveside for many minutes under a large umbrella and removed his hat as he stared down grief stricken as the coffin was lowered. The throng of relatives and other mourners then filed past to say their final goodbyes having to be regulated by the police into a single file to avoid accidents and it was half an hour before they all left the graveyard.

Two days later on the Sunday, crowds of people flocked to the little churchyard to see the spot where Mrs Luard was buried, while many more made a nuisance of themselves endeavouring to see the exact spot where she was murdered at the Casa by attempting to breakthrough the thinly spread police cordon that had been left on guard.

7

USELESS CLUES & WASTED TIME

The search for clues begins

'You can tell when all hope of solving a case has gone,' Edwin commented to Tom Gutteridge as he watched a man in a green cap with a black frock coat walking down the muddy track from the woods holding a piece of twisted wire in front of him.

'How's that? asked Tom?'

'When it's turned into a veritable circus.'

'I take it you mean that lot?'

'Indeed I do.'

'I think the Chief maybe clutching at straws.'

'Or clutching bits of wire,' Edwin chuckled.

'I take it then you are not a believer in such ethereal sciences,' commented Tom jokingly.

'Total rot in my opinion and it makes us look, well, like idiots in front of the press.'

'Yeh. I can imagine the headlines in the morning. I've read that it's a successful method for finding water sources.'

'Well, let's hope they don't just lead everybody to the fish ponds,' said Edwin sarcastically.

'At least it has given all our lot something to smirk about and the press more to write about.'

For some reason only known to the Warde, three diviners had been allowed to come down from Lancashire. Their leader, a Mr Berry, had told Edwin earlier that he attributed his powers to a combination of mind and metal, to which Edwin had difficulty keeping a straight face. His two companions who followed him wherever he went, extolled his powers, calling him the "human bloodhound," cue another smirk from Edwin.

Edwin and Tom had watched as Mr Berry had taken out two lengths of copper wire bent at the ends with half curves and headed off with his two assistants and Warde and his deputy Major Lafone in tow. The small band walked up the path taken by Mrs Luard towards the veranda. Suddenly Mr Berry detached himself from the others and strode onto the veranda coming to a sudden halt and then twiddled the wires violently which began to slowly move upwards to form a complete circle and Mr Berry watched them with staring eyes exclaiming to the Chief Constable, 'This is where the murderer stood!'

'God give us strength,' muttered the watching Edwin under his breath.

With his eyes closed, he twiddled the wires again which were balanced on the ends of his fingers and slowly walked from the veranda along a flattened path at the back of the Casa through the bracken which the police had followed days before. When they got near the fence, where the first search had lost the trail, the diviner stopped again, and the wires rotated and oscillated in "an alarming manner" according to those present. Then the diviner rushed off at speed with Warde and Lafone hurrying behind until they reached the St Lawrence churchyard near the Frankfield House. When they had disappeared into the distance Tom had turned to Edwin and asked, 'Aren't we going to follow?'

Edwin turned and gave him a sorrowful look, 'You are joking. Let's go and find a cup of tea.'

Later in an interview with the *Lloyd's News* special correspondent, Mr Berry said that "I had no difficulty in pointing out the position in which Mrs Luard was found. Then I was able to see in my mind's eye the whole tragedy. I could see, for instance, the position occupied by the murderer when he fired the first shot. Since then I have followed the exact route which the murderer took after he had committed the crime. I cannot disclose what I know, I wish I could. I mean that the footprints which the police found were certainly not those of the murderer.' When asked what he actually achieved he replied, 'I have solved the mystery!'

***

Edwin was expert enough to realise that without a large sliver of luck the case was heading towards unsolvable. The major problem was that they still had no prime suspect, no witnesses, no murder weapon and no obvious motive. How can you solve a case without at least one of these elements to go with. The search for the stolen jewellery had yielded no positive results even though many pawnbrokers from across the country were making reports of similar items being offered to them. Again this tied up officers in many areas checking the reports and on a few occasions seizing the jewellery and bringing it to Kent to be identified.

Many offers of practical help were also forthcoming, some taken up, others dismissed. Those accepted like the diviners kept the press in copy and provided amusement to many including Edwin. Another offer of help accepted by Warde was from a Major Richardson from Stratford-upon-Avon offering the services of his two "famous" bloodhounds named Solferino and Sceptre. The introduction of the dogs was viewed by many as another act of desperation, but Warde viewed it as a question of leaving no stone unturned. Most thought that there was little chance of them being of help because of the time lapse since the murder and the heavy rain which had fallen, probably obliterating any scent. The Major admitted that no bloodhound could find a footprint track after so long, but he would endeavour to find a scent. Bloodhounds had been trialled in some cities with alleged success, so it was not that unusual to make use of them.

On Wednesday 26 August, two days after the murder, the Major arrived at 8am at Wrotham station with his entourage and two dogs to much fanfare and excitement and were met by Scott and the Chief Constable. His arrival of course was leaked so a large contingent of journalists were present to report on this latest development. On reaching the Knoll they had breakfast and a large group consisting of Scott, Taylor, Sgt. Paramour and nine constables assembled and set off at 10am heading for the Casa. There was much excitement and an almost party atmosphere at this unusual turn of events.

Edwin and Tom watched from a distance until the group were out of sight and then Edwin turned to Tom and just uttered the words, 'a blimming circus.'

'I understand they have been trialled in London by the Yard and Scott has some belief in them.'

'He would, but seriously though the dogs might have been of some use if we'd had them within a few hours of the committal of the crime, but now there's no shred of anything from which they can get an initial scent. Like us they need something to go on.'

On reaching the bungalow the Major was shown the bloodstain on the veranda and Solferino became very stimulated, sniffing at doors and lingering in certain places before all of a sudden making for the back of the stable, and after a little hesitation then set off up a steep hill into the wood. The pursuing pack of officers had difficulty keeping up, stumbling on roots and snagging on bushes and it was a comical sight. The dogs seemed keen but after a hard struggle amid thick bracken they came to a dead halt, whatever they were following was lost.

A consultation took place between Major Richardson and Scott and it was decided to try the fields on the opposite side of the road in case the fugitive had made his way there. The dogs were then led into some paddocks but they seemed to take little interest in the place and this was given up. The Major realised it was a false trail and so they all trooped despondently back to the Casa where they tried again. Solferino began following the same trail, and was halted again, and they tried a third time. Eventually after an hour the Major left Sceptre behind and continued with one hound which he believed was on to something as it began to run through the wood barking. One of the party described afterwards that they "Slipped down a steep declivity, many of us stumbling over the soft, springy undergrowth."

After five hundred yards the Major sent for Sceptre again and the two dogs plunged on until they reached the Tonbridge Road where again they lost interest. It had been a waste of time, but the Major believed that because the dogs kept following the same trail they were on the track of a man who had bloodstains on his boots. He rather fancifully prophesised that the man walked the trail to the road hesitated and remained there out of sight until night fell and then went on to the road and disappeared. It was now noon and evidently the hunt had failed, man and beast were thirsty, and a visit was made to the local tavern where the party of man hunters attracted considerable attention from the regulars.

Scott later commented that dogs were only useful perhaps once in a hundred times but even this could be of value in certain circumstances and he was a believer himself in a bloodhound's powers as he had a good knowledge of that breed of dog. He recalled that Sir Charles Warren, when commissioner at Scotland Yard, experimented with bloodhounds but found them useless in the London streets. The Major though strongly insisted that Scotland Yard should now restart their experiments, but Scott pointed out that as the department was very seldom asked to interfere in these country crimes it wasn't worth persevering with. It was unclear to most people what they expected to achieve anyway so long after the incident.

***

Edwin was sitting in his office at Wrens Court in Maidstone staring out of the window and fuming. He had just finished reading an article in the *Courier* newspaper which was now lying on the floor in the corner of the room where he had thrown it. It was three weeks since the murder and the investigation was grinding on and he had to be honest, they were getting nowhere and the press had turned against the police. Tom Gutteridge appeared at the door at this point and could see that Edwin was not best pleased.

'What's up, Guv?'

'Have you read the Courier this morning?'

'Can't say I have. Something in there you didn't like I take it,' he said viewing the paper on the floor.

'You could say that. Pick it up will you.'

Tom bent and got the paper and handed it to Edwin.

'The paper thinks we were a bit tardy calling in the Yard,' Edwin told Tom.

'We expected something like that didn't we?'

'Well yes but listen to this: "The Yard are the finest detective band in the world. Every man is an expert who has won his spurs in numerous difficult cases within the metropolitan area. When murder or other important crimes take place the local detective inspector rushes to the scene by motor car within a very short time so that on his arrival he sees the clues while they are still hot and such evidence as there may be is still undisturbed." Have you ever heard such tosh?'

'Bit over the top I must say, but you know the press.'

'You haven't heard the best of it yet. This bit is what riles me, listen to this, "In country districts, the procedure is unfortunately very different. If a murder takes place in a country town or village, the superintendent or the chief constable in the ordinary course takes charge of the case and proceeds to the spot and directs the investigation. In the old recourse, it is only after these local officials, whose experience in dealing with serious crime is naturally very limited, find themselves in difficulties that the assistance of Scotland Yard is applied for. By that time, the criminal has had a good start and these inexpert local men have trodden or failed to note what should have been seized on.'

'What a cheek!' exclaimed Tom.

'Exactly. Its damned insulting, "limited experience" indeed and "inexpert local men trampling everywhere." Who do they think we are. You wait until I see their reporter next.' Edwin glowered.

'In fairness to the Chief he did call them within twenty-four hours of the murder and called us straight away.'

'Exactly. And I might point out that Scott and Savage haven't brought much to the case. "Every man an expert" he read again. 'Tosh.'

Edwin could not see anything else that he or his officers could have done better. From the start they had asked from the public any sightings of strangers acting suspiciously within a three-mile radius of the scene of the murder on the Monday afternoon. There had been quite a response and officers had been furnished with descriptions of these persons. So far as these individuals could be traced, they were able to satisfy them that they had nothing to do with the crime. Strenuous efforts had been made to trace the missing rings. On Monday evening, 31 August a Birmingham detective accompanied by Chief Inspector Scott arrived at Sevenoaks with two rings in his possession that had been pawned. The two officers took them to the General but he failed to identify them. The servants at the Knoll also didn't recognise them. A London pawnbroker in Hoxton came forward with rings which he thought corresponded with the published description and again they were duly brought to the General with the same result. And so it had gone on. They were just not having any luck.

Ten days after the murder Scott asked Edwin if he would help him ascertain whether the three shots several witnesses had reported were in fact as audible as they claimed. The question had arisen whether these were really revolver shots or shots from a rifle being used by a sportsman. They arranged for three shots to be fired at the Casa from a revolver which used the same cartridges at an arranged time while Edwin and Scott stood at the same spot three hundred yards away where Mrs Wickham had stood. Both men heard the shots distinctly and both agreed that they would have been audible a great deal further away.

No gun had been found and it was likely that the murderer after firing had kept the gun and thrown it when he was well away from the scene. The hunt to find the gun had been abandoned just the day before Scott had arrived from London with the gun expert.

Despite the lack of a lead they hadn't given up. The Chief had put out an appeal for information across the nation and it had backfired spectacularly when they were literally inundated with letters, telegrams and walk ins from people offering theories, information and their services. It was extremely difficult to sort the wheat from the chaff but the Chief was insistent that every snippet of information was followed up. Most of these were of little use and in some cases absurd, or as the *Sevenoaks Chronicle* put it:

> Day and night Supt. Taylor has followed clues and made inquiries into the various issues. He has received dozens of letters, some sensible, many more idiotic, but all this means work for the officials, and in a good number of cases useless work which entails the waste of valuable time.

The whole force was occupied reading all the missives preventing them from carrying out their normal duties, but the murder obviously took priority. Not a day passed without someone being detained on suspicion or detectives sent on fool's errand's to interview obvious time wasters and cranks. The press reported that the police had been:

> hampered by individuals who have in some cases been thoughtless and others, it is to be feared, maliciously bombarded them with suggestions. They have even had communication from clairvoyants who have been seen the crime enacted in a vision and have furnished elaborate and purely fanciful descriptions of the author of the crime. The few persons who have come under the band of suspicion have speedily, on being questioned, been able to prove their incontestable innocence, and at present there is no one under observation whom the police suspect of having any knowledge. Of the tragic episode in the wood there will, of course, be no relaxation of their efforts in the disheartening and thankless task in which they are now engaged. But the murderer, so far as the present outlook goes, has seemingly vanished and left no trace.

Some of the hoaxes were initially viewed as possibly having some credence. On the 14 September a coat and pair of boots was found on the banks of Regents Park Lake with a note attached: "*My Dear father, I can bear the suspense no longer. The Ightham affair has preyed on my mind. I fired the shots while the devil was in me. By the time you get this I shall be beyond all human help. Your unfortunate son, Jack Storm.*" This resulted in the authorities trawling the lake for a body and Edwin having to go to London to attend. It turned out to be a hoax and no such Jack Storm existed. George Robert Sims, journalist, poet, dramatist, novelist and bon vivant who lived near the lake wrote in his column in *The Daily Mail*:

> In the warm soft air of the sweet September morning, I stood on the romantic little bridge by the lake in Regent's Park and peered into the quiet waters which has suddenly become the new centre of interest in the tragedy of the Kentish Woods. The dragging of the lake in search of the body of the man who had, in a letter left upon the bank, proclaimed himself the murderer of Mrs Luard, had been abandoned until certain alterations could be made to the drags. I crossed the road to my home convinced that this latest phase of the haunting mystery was but a gruesome trick with a morbid and mischievous sense of humour.

The last three weeks had been a tiring, frustrating and busy. Edwin and Gutteridge had travelled the length and breadth of Kent and London following up leads all of which proved to be to no avail, but they had kept at it even though they knew each one was a thankless task. On September 4 they were in London investigating the writer of a letter sent to the General claiming that he had murdered Mrs Luard "for revenge after waiting for three years." When Edwin read it he could see immediately that it was written by an illiterate or disguised hand and the journey was going to be fruitless. And it was. After interviewing him it turned out to be another hoax.

Then there was the report that at about 6pm on the afternoon of the murder a man allegedly entered the tavern in the village of Larkfield, agitated and trembling violently, and asked for a brandy and then proceeded to offer a ring for sale at five shillings but received no takers as fellow drinkers believed it to be worthless.

News had not spread at that time of the murder and stolen rings. Rumours suggested that this man headed for Maidstone where a bargeman working by the Medway bridge saw a man toss a revolver into the river. More rumours then spread that a diver from London was being sourced to search for it, which of course absurd.

In another incident a labourer walked into Tonbridge police station and informed them that while passing Crown Point at about 4pm on the Monday afternoon, he saw a man, apparently of the outdoor work artisan class, coming from a wood near the scene. He gave a description, and Edwin's detectives made enquiries in the area but it came to nothing.

Then on Sunday 30 August their luck seemed to be changing with a report of a more positive nature. They received news that a man, who professed to have lost his memory, had been admitted to the Pembury Workhouse, a massive institution just outside Tunbridge Wells, which regularly held five hundred inmates. The man had been one of a hundred short stay casual "walk ins," that the workhouse took in during the busy summer.

Under interrogation he told an elaborate story that while on a cycling excursion in the Ightham area he suddenly had a memory loss and found himself at Paddock Wood railway station without his bike and unable to remember anything. He walked to Tonbridge and found a constable Horton and told him his problem. Horton escorted him to the workhouse to be put under observation.

When Horton mentioned the encounter to his sergeant, alarm bells rang and Taylor was informed that the man had been in the area of the murder, and at the time of it, immediately put him under suspicion. On Sunday afternoon, Taylor and Edwin went to the workhouse to interview the suspect. He was unable to give his name and had no identification on him. The two officers asked him questions about London in order to ascertain whether he was feigning his memory loss. He was able to describe every part of London but still maintained that he knew absolutely nothing about himself. Edwin was not convinced and suggested to Taylor that they kept him under surveillance while they obtained medical opinion. Detective Everett of Tonbridge police was assigned to keep the man under supervision until they could discover who he was. The next day they returned with Doctor Taylor, the Malling Division medical officer who examined him and he remained quite convincing and still adhered to his story.

Eventually the man, who was shamming, realised he might be accused of murder so he admitted to Everrett that everything he had said was false and he had only done it to get into the workhouse. He was in fact twenty-eight-year-old Alfred Pearson, a dairy manager of 250 High Street, Tottenham described as of a bad character and wanted by police in London. He made a long statement in writing. When asked why he had acted in such a strange way and wasted their time he just said that he didn't want anyone to discover he was a wanted man and he had no idea that his behaviour would make detectives think he had anything to do with the Ightham murder. Although he apologised for all the trouble he caused he didn't avoid being charged with making a false statement for the purpose of obtaining relief at the Tonbridge Union Workhouse, and for being guilty of disorderly conduct by malingering on 29-31 August on the basis that he stated he had no knowledge of where he was or doing the afternoon of murder. He was sentenced to 14 days with hard labour. Supt Taylor and Edwin were satisfied he was in no way connected with the murder.

Hopes were then raised again the next day on Monday 31 August when while on duty at the Admiralty pier in Dover, a week after the murder, an observant police constable named Spinner noticed a man lounging about whose appearance exactly tallied with an official wanted notice that had been issued for a man seen coming from the Seal Chart woods on the day of the murder. *The Morning Post* described him as of the labouring class with a pronounced squint in his right eye and red hair and beard. The eager officer immediately detained him already imagining the kudos he would get if this turned out to be the wanted murderer. Spinner became even more animated when he discovered his prisoner had associations with the Luard family. He was taken to Dover police station and Edwin and Supt. Taylor rushed there in high spirits to interview him where the prisoner divulged that he had a home at Ightham and had worked for the General as a gardener until they had quarrelled, and he was sacked. Both officers became extremely excited as they thought, this was the stroke of luck they had been waiting for and they had their man. There exhilaration was heightened when the man told them he had been discharged from General Luard's employment following an argument and had been tramping the country with occasional calls at his Ightham home. Unfortunately yet again their hopes were dashed when he was able to substantiate an alibi of being in another part of Kent for the day of the murder.

8

THE LUARD TRAGEDY

Major-General Charles Luard, R.E., F.R.G.S., J.P.

In the days following his wife's death there was a swell of public sympathy for the widowed General both locally and across the nation which was demonstrated in a flood of letters and telegrams.

He was quite overcome emotionally by this response and although still grieving greatly, he endeavoured to answer as many as he could. One such letter that must have brought some comfort to him was from a former housemaid who told a *Courier* reporter:

> A more devoted couple, it was almost impossible to see and a kinder master and mistress I have never had. When I heard of Mrs Luard's death, I wrote to the General expressing my deep sympathy in his terrible bereavement, and a fortnight ago received an autograph letter back from him thanking me very kindly for my sympathy. His concluding words being that Captain Luard, his son, was expected in England on September 19 and the comfort it would bring to him. I hardly expected that after so many years out of his employ I should have received an answer to my letter, but almost immediately he had replied. I have that letter and shall keep it as a sad memento of an honourable man and a distinguished soldier, a man incapable of a dishonourable action let alone the dastardly deed attributed to him by those who stab in the dark and ought to be severely punished for so doing.

So many letters and telegrams arrived that he was forced eventually to resort to asking the Editor of the *Sevenoaks Chronicle,* the main local newspaper to print a thank you letter from him:

> I should be very much obliged, if you will permit me, through your columns, to acknowledge the very large number of telegrams, letters and cards which I have recently received expressing such deep sympathy for me. The public at large has been deeply disturbed by this awful crime, and

> I may have some rights to ask if the time has not ride for clearing away from our roads, our lanes, and our woods, the many thousands of unemployed people, many of them in a desperate state from want that might give way to temptation and commit the worst of sins. I am, Dear Sir, Yours Truly, C.E Luard, Major General, Ightham Knoll, 8th of September 1908.

Initially these were pleasant condolence letters both from the general public and his friends. He spent hours personally answering them, but the worst aspect of this deluge of correspondence was that as the days went by the contents turned more sinister and he began to receive hate mail. He also received messages from person's claiming to be the murderer. All this correspondence was passed onto the police and suggestions made in these anonymous letters were also being sent direct to the coroner. The police, of course, were bound to act on them, and detectives were dispatched to investigate the claims of the writers.

Many of the hate communications had local postmarks and this was the worst ignominy as he had always believed he was liked and respected in the community as both he and his wife had done everything they could to be of service to them. It was the worst dishonour and hit him hard particularly those that besmirched the name of his wife suggesting the murderer was a lover and that the meeting at the bungalow was no chance one but an assignation. One commentator, rather uncharitably, scotched this thought by quoting a line from Hamlet: "Reason and such facts as are known, however, tell against any thought of a liaison. Mrs Luard's years are against it at such an age as hers, '"the heyday in the blood is tame, it is humble."'

He also became aware of some of the awful insinuations being discussed in whispers around the district that he was having an affair rather than playing golf, that he was the murderer and encouraging him to give himself up or commit suicide. All these missives were ultimately destroyed.

He could not bring himself to stay in the house surrounded by memories of Caroline and was already making tentative arrangements to leave the neighbourhood and distance himself from the tragic events. His many friends rallied round and endeavoured to cheer him and take his mind off the tragedy by inviting him to stay with them. He would spend the day time packing up the house helped by his staff and then travel to wherever he was staying the night. He spent some nights at the Army and Navy club, in Piccadilly, London and in Cumbria with his half-brother. He stayed with his closest neighbour and friend Sir William Boord and his wife who lived opposite in Oldbury Place and with the Colyer-Fergusons at his old family home of Ightham Mote and the Collets at St Clere house. He accepted so many invites that he didn't spend another night in the house after her death.

He placed for sale notices in several London morning newspapers: "Ightham Knoll, near Sevenoaks. Eight years of lease can be transferred; house, stable, cottage and eight acres. Rent £200." The agent responsible was Hampton's who commented "The General is very anxious to be rid of the place. In addition we are selling the furniture and contents with a few exceptions by auction on 24 September."

One of his closest friends was Colonel Charles "Charlie" Edward Warde, the brother of the Chief Constable, and M.P. for Medway. He was in Wales when he heard of the tragic event that had befallen his good friend and neighbour and he quickly caught a train home to support him. On arrival he had driven over to

Ightham Knoll and taken the General for a drive in the countryside and they talked of anything but the loss of his wife. When they got back to the Knoll he was invited in for tea and they sat in the drawing room and continued their conversation.

They sat in silence for a while Charlie looked out the bay window at the lawn and then surveyed the room before commenting, 'Have you given thought to your future plans?'

The General replied dismally, 'As you know I can't bear staying overnight here. All my friends have been so kind to me, and I have not slept in the house once since her death. There is no future for me here unfortunately.'

'So you are thinking of moving from the area altogether?'

'I'm afraid so. I see no alternative. I am thinking of taking furnished rooms over my club as an interim measure.'

'It goes without saying that you are welcome at Barham Court. I would be glad if you could spare at least a day to stay with me before you leave for good.'

'That is a kind offer Charlie, and I will certainly keep that in mind.'

'What will you do with the house and furniture?'

'I am packing up everything that my son may wish and most of the furniture will be sold.'

'Are you sure. That seems such a shame after all these years.'

'But that's the point. Everything will remind me of my dear Daisy and all the happy times we had here. I may put in store the family sideboard and Caroline's writing desk if I can bear it.'

'You really must come and see us at Barham before you go,' Charlie insisted.

'Well, I hope to have all the packing done by Tuesday. The staff have been so helpful, and I will be so sorry to leave them. Then I will be visiting a dear friend in London from Wednesday. I must then meet my son off the ship in Southampton on Saturday. I am looking forward to seeing him but I so wish the circumstances were different.'

'I can perfectly understand that, but don't worry I will be by your side.'

'Oh Charlie that is so thoughtful, but you needn't you know.'

'I insist Charles. It is not a journey to do on your own.'

'I can't thank you enough for your kindness.'

'We are old friends aren't we? You would do the same for me.'

'I will let you know when I will arrive to stay before we go to Southampton.'

'That will be fine. Make sure you do.'

Charlie left the house and walked to his car in a worried mood as he had never seen his friend in such a despondent state and was determined to try and lighten his mindset when he came to stay.

***

The General eventually sent a telegram on the 15 September to Charlie from London saying: "Will come with pleasure for Thursday night. Can you send motor, six o'clock Thursday?'

Charlie was much relieved to receive the message and collected him in his car from the Knoll on the Thursday afternoon as requested. As they left the house they stopped to take in the "most brilliant sunset the two of them had ever seen" and kept talking about it along the way. Charlie thought his friend's manner was "absolutely quiet and natural," with no indication of any ill thoughts.

On arrival at Barham Court the General was greeted by Helen, Charlie's wife, and taken to his room by the butler James Wolff and allowed to settle in before going down to the drawing room. The Luards had visited the mansion countless times over the years and all the staff were familiar with them and loved the couple. All of them were upset about Caroline's death and found it difficult not to show it in their faces but they were under orders from their master to treat the General as normally as possible. James had known the couple for four years so like everyone else was upset by the circumstances particularly as Mrs Luard had always been kind to him. He was quite concerned about the General's appearance since the last time he had seen him saying later that "his face was considerably drawn showing the unusual experience he had gone through, but apart from that he appeared to be, I might say, cheerful."

At dinner there was no way of avoiding the question of the upcoming inquest hearing which Charlie was getting irritated about due to the stress being caused to his friend.

'Why do they keep adjourning the inquest?' asked Charlie.

'I wish I knew my friend.'

'I see no reason why it cannot be concluded. The police can still continue their investigation.'

'I agree, I wish they would. I do not want to have to go back . I wrote to Tom Buss asking him if I could be excused. He sent me a very courteous letter saying questions might arise which made it necessary.'

'Preposterous. It seems jolly cruel to keep distressing you in this way.'

'Some of the infernal questions they asked me at the last one were damn scandalous.'

'I dare say.'

Helen changed the subject to something more general and the three ate their meal. Charlie noticed that the General ate quite well but looked very tired and he noticed him yawn two or three times.

'How tiring your packing must have made you,' he said.

'I am tired, but I cannot sleep anyway.'

'Do you think it was wise to have packed up in such a hurry,' inquired Helen kindly.

'My two brother-in-laws and sister-in-law were unanimous in agreeing with me that it might be the best thing to do.'

'Where will you go?' asked Helen.

'A friend of mine is lending me a house in Dulverton in Somersetshire, and I intend taking my son there.'

'That sounds wonderful.'

Helen said goodnight and they went to Charlie's study and sat talking, drinking brandy and smoking for a while longer and then Charlie escorted him to his room. At the door he said, 'Good night dear friend. Try and get some rest. What time would you like to be called and have breakfast?'

'Please call me at eight if you don't mind.'

'Would you like to have tea first thing in your room?'

'Thank you, yes.'

'And a bath.,

'You are spoiling me.'

'Hot or cold?'

'Hot most definitely! Goodnight Charlie,' he said with a smile and closed the door.

***

The General awoke about 8am and lazed in bed. At ten past eight there was a knock at the door, and he called out, "Come in."

Bernard Kelly, the footman entered with a tray on which was a cup of tea and some bread and butter.

'Good morning sir, I hope you slept well. I have a cup of tea for you.'

'That's splendid, just put it on the bedside table will you.'

Bernard did as he was told and was obviously aware of the circumstances bringing the General there so looked closely at him to see his demeanour so he could report back to the other staff, but he appeared quite cheerful.

'Is there anything else I can do for you?'

'No. I will dress myself in a minute.'

Having finished his tea he got out of bed, had a bath and methodically got dressed and donned a black lounge suit. He left the guest bedroom holding his bowler hat. As he descended the staircase a maid was heading upstairs, and she curtsied, and they exchanged cordial greetings. He then headed to the kitchen which surprised the cook and kitchen maid although the General was known to be informal with house staff.

'Is there anything we can do for you, sir?'

'No, everything is fine. I am just going to have a stroll round the garden before breakfast to get my appetite up.'

They watched as he donned his hat and let himself out the kitchen door. He stopped to take in the pleasant pastoral scene in front of him of the estate with sheep grazing on the grass and all the autumn-coloured trees stretching into the distance. He walked briskly down the long drive looking from side to side until he reached the South Lodge gate where Robert Wright the gate keeper was busy sweeping up the autumn leaves. He paused as the General approached and gave him a salute.

"Good morning, sir,' the General said to Robert.

The gatekeeper somewhat perplexed by being addressed as sir replied, 'Good morning to you, sir.'

The General continued his walk watched with interest by the gatekeeper who thought it was strange he was heading up the road and not taking a stroll round the garden before breakfast. The General turned into Farleigh Road and walked fifty yards to a five barred gate on his right-hand side. Without hesitation he clambered rather awkwardly over the gate and up and over a grassy mound along a farmer's track that led down to a level crossing situated between the villages of East Farleigh and Wateringbury on the railway line from Maidstone to Sevenoaks. He stood for a while at the top of the mound and looked out over the beautiful undulating scenery of orchards and hop fields and the quietly flowing Medway with its well wooded banks and the foliage now in all its glory of first Autumn tints. How he loved the Garden of England.

The crossing, known as Chalk Rough, was straight in front of him and only used by local farmers to reach their fields the other side of the line and the River Medway which runs parallel. The gate was kept locked not being a public right of way and the local farmers each had a key. Having rambled the surrounding countryside of the Barham estate many times he was aware of the level crossing. He stopped half way down a slope and kept watch up and down the line. He noticed a man on the bank of the river washing himself and then continued observing the rail track.

Patrick Cale, a hop picker, was making use of the river for his ablutions which he did every morning at about the same time and rarely if ever saw anyone. He was well aware of the times the trains passed by and when he heard a whistle looked up to watch. He then spotted an old gentleman formally dressed standing a few yards from the track which he thought rather strange but continued watching the approaching train. It was the 9.12am from Maidstone to Paddock Wood and as it came almost level he saw the old gentleman hurry towards the line and calmly jump in front of it. He could not help himself from screaming at the sight. Later he commented, 'Of course, I could not see what happened to him at the moment of impact because the train shut off my view, but I knew the gentleman must have been killed.'

Frederick Bridges, the unfortunate train driver, had spotted the man next to the line as he came round the curve approaching the crossing and sounded the whistle. The man appeared to ignore it, so he sounded it again twice but was aghast to see him cross the other line and step towards his train. He looked on in horror as he put both hands over his face and walked calmly in front of the train. Frederick saw him "cut in halves" and fall dead in front of him as the train passed him by. He had no chance of pulling up as they were travelling at fifty miles an hour but he slammed on the brake lever and let out the steam as soon as he could and there was a grinding screech as the wheels tried to grip and a loud hiss of steam, but the train took a while to come to rest. Several of the passengers were thrown about from their seats, believing the train had crashed.

Cale had stood stupefied for a while at the horror of what he had just witnessed but soon gathered his nerve and ran over to the line. In many ways he wished he hadn't as the horrific sight of the General's blooded body almost cut in half lying beside the track was a sight that would remain with him all his life. He looked round at a loss as to what to do next but luckily he saw two railway workers running along the line towards him with the guard and driver in tow.

Richard Hoper, a signalman, was a few hundred yards down the track chatting to a group of platelayers when the train finally came to a stop beside them. Frederick shouted to him, 'I think we've hit a man.' Richard looked at the foreman trying to decide what to do, but the leader of the gang told two of his men to run up the line sent to see if they could help in any way. Again they recoiled in horror at the half-dressed mangled body of the man. The train driver and guard arrived, and Frederick collapsed in shock and was tended to by the guard.

Meanwhile the signalman had rushed off to Teston village not far away in search of the local bobby and luckily quickly found him. Richard was in a state of panic, but Constable James Masters, calmed him and followed Richard back to the scene. The constable searched the remnants of the clothing, while the others watched, and found a laundry mark in the name of C E Luard. In a pocket he also found an envelope with a message scribbled on it. It said, "General Luard's body to be taken to Colonel Warde's, Barham Court, 18-9-08."

'Kind of the gentleman to let us know who he is. Someone better go and fetch a cart.'

The body parts were wrapped in a tarpaulin from the signal box and carried as reverently as possible under the circumstances back up the hill towards the estate.

***

Meanwhile Charlie was sitting in the dining room with Helen waiting for the General to come down for breakfast totally oblivious to all the events that were unfolding. It was unusual for him not to be punctual or discourteous, so Charlie was worried. He sent for Wolff.

'Have you any idea where our guest is, Wolff?'

'No sir, but the kitchen staff told me earlier he went out for a walk.'

'Rather strange, without telling us. Can you see if you can find him.'

The butler checked round the immediate garden without success and came back into the house checking all the downstair rooms before going up to the bedroom. The door was ajar, so he looked in but it was empty. Wolf hurried back to his master to give him the news. Charlie then got up from the table and informed Helen that he would check outside himself. As he began to walk up the drive he was astonished to see an obviously out of breath Constable Marsh hurrying towards him.

'Whatever is the matter, constable?' he asked.

'A body has been found on the railway line sir. It's a terrible sight if I may say so. I found a note on it signed C. E. Luard saying to inform you.'

'Good God man, no, this is awful! ' exclaimed Charlie, 'Come in constable for a minute, you look exhausted.

'I am a bit unsettled sir.'

'Wolff, get the constable a drink,' he shouted, 'Wait here constable.'

Charlie went into the dining room and gave his wife the news. She gasped and covered her mouth with her hand and he told her, 'I must go and see what is happening.'

Charlie went into the hall to find the now recovered constable, 'You had better take me to the scene.'

The two marched quickly up the drive watched by Wolff who being a conscientious butler thought for a moment what was best to do and went up to the guest bedroom again to search it. He spotted three letters on the writing bureau. The top one was addressed to his master, one for Captain Luard, his son and the other to Mr Hartley, the brother-in-law. The General's watch and chain, keys and a pile of money were also there. He quickly locked the room put the key in his pocket and ran after his master eventually catching up with him and gave him the letter.

Having thanked Wolff for his efforts he carried on with the constable, reading the letter as he went, getting more distressed at what he was reading:

My Dear Warde. I am sorry to have returned your kindness in hospitality and long friendship in this way. But I am satisfied that it is best to join her in the Second Life at once, and so I can be of no further use to anyone in the future in this world of which I am tired and which I do not wish to live any longer. I thought my strength was sufficient to bear up against the horrible imputations and terrible letters I have received, since that awful crime was committed, which robbed me of all my happiness. And so it was the goodness, kindness and simply having so many friends which kept one going, but somehow now, in the last day or two, something seems to have snapped. The strength has left me, and I care for nothing except to join her again. So goodbye, dear friend, to both of you, to both of us, yours very affectionately. C.E Luard.

PS I shall be somewhere on the line of the railway. Please send off enclosed three telegrams to Elmhirst, to my brother-in-law T Hartley and my maid.

Having finished the letter, he was devastated and could not take it in. How could his friend have done such a thing. Charles and the constable met up with the cart as it approached the South Lodge and he quickly identified the body as the General. He then supervised the body being placed in the unoccupied Lodge and made it secure. He then hurried to his friend's room, unlocked it and opened the closed shutters as it was dark. The footman had informed him that he had seen the General at 8.10am when he took the tea to him. He found that the tea had been drunk and the bread and butter eaten, then checked the sponge and towel which were damp so he must have bathed. Charlie stood and tried to ponder what had occurred in the room overnight and that morning which would lead to his friend committing such an act. He was having difficulty understanding the General's actions as he had previously accepted Charlie's offer of accompanying him to Southampton, was looking forward to seeing his son and told him that he wanted a car to take him there at 11am. He had also planned on taking his silver plate to his London bank before continuing to Southampton. These actions did not feel like a man planning a suicide and he could only conclude that "something had snapped" as the General had declared and it was a last-minute decision.

Standing in the room he tried to imagine what the General had done before leaving on his fatal walk. He would have had to drink his tea, eat the bread, have a bath, get dressed and write the letters all in the space of thirty-five to forty minutes if the maid was correct in the time she passed him on the stairs at 8.45am. Unless of course he had written the letters and telegrams the night before. But this did not make any sense to him. The General had said he couldn't sleep and therefore could have spent all night writing them, but he noticed that the brand-new candles he had given him the previous evening were only burned down a quarter of an inch. They had only been alight a very short time, probably not long enough to write the letters.

The first senior officer to arrive was Superintendent Ford and his first task was to search the bedroom and make a note of all the General's belongings. These included a pair of spectacles, a pipe, tobacco pouch, two pencils, 32 penny stamps, 12 half-penny stamps, a gold watch and chain, a locket, compass, two bunches of keys, some change, a telegram form torn in six pieces and a photograph and letter to his son. When the torn telegram was pieced together they discovered it was to his brother-in-law and read, "Something has snapped. My strength has gone. I have gone to join her. I had left her everything but have now made a new will leaving everything to my son and you as sole executor. Goodbye dear brother, ever yours, P.S. It is all the horrid letters and insinuations which have been made."

The news soon reached London and spread across the country as yet another sensational story and twist to the murder resurrecting more rumours and theories. One with more compassion than others was George R Sims, journalist and novelist who wrote about the breaking news in the *Daily Mail:*

> Men of this world, as the first news came through with scant detail, ask themselves in amazement if it were possible that this disaster upon disaster could be the result of accident. And the first impressions slowly shaped itself to the terrible word that ultimately proved to be the keynote of the tragedy. As I sped swiftly through the London streets in the early afternoon on my way to the scene of the last startling act in this mysterious real-life drama, the newspaper stand content bills bore one legend alone. "General Luard Dead!" But suddenly a headline struck my eyes as with a blow which said "Suicide of General Luard! The words seemed almost cruel as they stood out blackly in the sunshine. Alas, they did not but tell the brief and bitter truth. The heartbroken man who but a few weeks ago had found the body of his murdered wife lying in the veranda of the summer house where he had earlier in the day left her full of life and happiness had deliberately gone to his self-planned death."

***

There was no rest for poor Charlie and his wife who through no fault of their own found themselves at the epicentre of this second tragedy and having to cope with the aftermath. He was experiencing the mental and physical consequences of his friend's actions, having to calm an upset staff, suffering his house being invaded with police and his property under siege from the press.

And there was plenty more to do. On Friday he travelled down to Southampton by train to meet his friend's son who was arriving early next morning on the Union Castle Line ship SS Norman from South Africa where he was stationed with his regiment. He was obviously expecting to be greeted by his father. Special arrangements had been made in conjunction with the shipping line to inform him of his father's death as gently as possible. The Company had sent a letter with the pilot requesting that the ship's doctor, J. W. Smith, should inform Captain Elmhirst Luard of his father's demise as compassionately as he could, but without giving him any particulars.

When the ship reached the quayside just after 4am, the gangway was run out and Charlie and Mr Langley the superintendent of the Union Castle Line went on board. They were taken to the son's large cabin at once, where they found Doctor Smith keeping the tanned thirty-year old company and there Charlie broke the sad news of the manner in which his father met his death. Elmhirst was distraught, and Charlie did his best to console him. He had arranged to travel back to London on the boat train, but it wasn't leaving for a couple of hours, and they had decided to stay ensconced in the cabin away from everyone, but Sir (Major) John Willoughby 5th. Baronet was travelling on the ship and had been aware of what was happening. He had previously arranged a private carriage to be attached to the mail train to convey him to London. He offered to accommodate Charlie and Elmhirst so they could be in private which they readily agreed to. The mail train was to leave soon, two hours earlier than the boat train and Custom officials fast tracked enough personal luggage to allow the captain a quick exit.

The train steamed out at 5.45am, and Elmhirst sat in silence with his face partly covered by his hands while Charlie gave him the full details of his father's horrific death and he apparently "took the news very bravely and now knew the worst." After leaving the station, he handed Elmhirst a package left by his father for him. On reaching Waterloo Station they then took a taxi to the Euston Hotel where they had breakfast. Later they took the train to Sevenoaks and on to Barham Court where at Charles's insistence he had been offered respite for as long as he wished.

***

The inquest took place at 3pm on Saturday afternoon in the Teston Parish Hall just three miles from Maidstone. Long before this a large a gathering of villagers, photographers and journalists, had collected to view a scene never before seen in the small hamlet, and which caused great excitement. Many stood in awe of the large collection of fine motor cars and carriages lined up along the lane. They stared at the policemen standing guard outside the door not allowing them to take a peek.

The centre of the hall had been allocated for the press and a large number of tables had been placed together to form a long row. Over forty pressmen finally sat there. Before proceedings began the jury were conveyed in a horse drawn shooting break to the South Lodge for the unenviable task of viewing the body, or what was left of it.

The busy Thomas Buss was seated on a platform at the end of the hall along with the Chief Constable, his deputy Lafone, Charlie Warde, Dr. Southwell Sanders the doctor who had examined the body and two of the General's relatives, Mr Luard Selby who resided at Ightham Mote and Mr Hartley his brother-in-law.

At the opening of the proceedings Mr Pullman, the Mayor of Maidstone, had managed to infiltrate the proceedings on the pretext of making a statement of condolence of behalf of the whole district:

> Will you allow me to say how greatly Maidstone, as the capital of Kent, is grieved by the tragic events which have been happening in this County, and to express the sympathy of the town with the relatives of General Luard and we commend Colonel Charles Warde whose natural kindness of heart prompted him to befriend the late General Luard in the time of his great grief.

The most dramatic and pathetic moment of the afternoon was when Elmhirst, who had only been aware of his father's death for a few hours, was summoned. There was a long pause before he appeared in the hall which had fallen eerily quiet. He entered looking worn and sad, with his face tense, and sat down next to the coroner. One newspaper described him as "tall, fair and handsome, with a pale moustache and wearing a blue lamb suit, his face calm and set in the sort of way which revealed a powerful will." He made quite an impression as he strode with firm steps across the room. It seemed unfair and cruel to put him through more trauma, but he was required to open the sealed letter written to him by his father just before his death in case there was something pertinent in it.

Thomas Buss melodramatically passed him the letter and there was complete silence and tangible expectancy as he broke the seal. The envelope contained two letters and a ring which fell to the floor accompanied by gasp from the onlookers as the captain retrieved it. He removed several sheets of aptly black edged paper and began reading them to himself. The silence continued as he went through the last words of his father slowly, without visible emotion. This done, he passed it back remarking that it did not contain anything of interest to the inquiry. This proved a disappointment to many present, but they held their breath again when Thomas Buss read the letter for himself and agreed. Once again a few were disappointed, but most were relieved that the confidence of its contents had been retained.

Dr Southwell Sanders related the horrific details of his examination of the body which made several present wince. The lower part was much mutilated, but the upper part was free from wounds, with the exception of the head, the left side of which was completely crushed as far as the angle of the left eye. Both arms were broken, the right in two places and his death was instantaneous which again was greeted with relief.

Bernard Kelly and James Wolff the butler gave evidence and Frederick Bridges; the train driver gave a harrowing and dramatic account of the moment of impact.

'I saw this gentleman coming towards the engine. I gave two sharp whistles to warn him but he kept on coming. He suddenly put his hands up in the air like this,' Fred held up his arms above his head to illustrate the point and continued, 'and fell down in front of the engine. I slammed on the brakes but he was too sharp for me. I did not knock him down. He fell, and I ran over him. It was a deliberate act.'

He was followed by Charles Warde. It was obvious that the Colonel was still greatly upset and was overcome several times as he related the events of the evening and the morning of the tragedy but managed to speak with "clear and straightforward military precision." Having answered all the questions put to him, he asked Thomas Buss if he would allow him to make a personal statement which was agreed. He then passionately made some personal observations on the events and became very animated waving his hands about, heatedly declaring that the General's actions were definitely unpremeditated and as proof of this he described how the General had a bath and drank a cup of tea, actions which did not lend itself to be a man in sound mind planning his own death. It was obvious something had snapped within him.

This part of his tirade was greeted with some disbelief by many present who were contemplating that the General's calm and organised activities were the exact opposite and akin to a planned and well executed military operation even arriving at the point of his demise at the right time to meet the train.

He then continued his diatribe to admonish the press for falsely publishing a letter purporting to be written by the General which contained a sentence stating he could not face his son. He was adamant that there was no such sentence in the letter that had been left to him by the General.

After the inquest Elmhirst wrote an open letter to the press for publication no doubt at Charlie's behest via the family solicitor Messrs. Key, Clark and Key of Sackville Street also admonishing them for the false letter and *The Globe* was one that apologised saying:

> It was proved at the inquest an absolute fabrication and no such letter was written by General Luard and he never said he could not face his son. The true contents of the last letter written by the late General to Colonel Warde were proved in the course of evidence given at the coroner's inquest on the 19th. The Globe newspaper was one of those that printed this letter, so we need hardly say how much we regret that we should have been misled into publishing so unfounded a statement which naturally gave deep pain to General Luard's, relatives and friends.

Thomas Buss began his summing up by recounting the events of the General's military career and then surprisingly moved on to make quite a controversial statement about intimations that the General had murdered his wife by saying:

> I think it is my duty to make some kind of reference to the many reports and baseless insinuations that had been made in the form of anonymous letters which had been sent to the General suggesting almost that he was responsible for the death of his wife. These letters have been innumerable and received by the police and by me in any number. But I need hardly tell you I have simply put them in the waste paper basket and have been disgusted with them. It is a feature of English justice, and we hope it will ever remain so, that until a man is found to be guilty of any crime, we must assume him to be innocent. Persons who have been prompted to write these letters have not been satisfied to let the General remain with his grief and sympathise with him in his great trouble but have added to the poignancy of his grief; and I imagine that, sensitive and honourable man that he was, it made his life almost unbearable. That, no doubt, was a great factor in inducing him to rid himself of this present life, and as he said, join his wife.
>
> Let us hope that the writers of these letters, if they have any conscience at all, will reflect and find that at any rate they must have contributed more or less to the doom to which the General sent himself. Let us hope, that although they treated him so badly in the last remaining days of his life they will, at any rate, respect his memory now and utter no more of these libellous and baseless and unfounded insinuations.

Thomas Buss had attracted much criticism himself from the press, the General's friends and the General himself for dragging his wife's inquest through three hearings and insisting he attended for more questioning causing him unnecessary distress. He took the opportunity at the end of his summing up to justify his actions:

> With regard to the questions, I asked General Luard at the inquest. I have no reason to defend my conduct in any way. I am not responsible to anyone in that particular matter. But I would like to say that, having regard to the rumours that were in circulation after the first sitting of the inquest, the suggestions that the General knew something about this unfortunate affair, I felt it my duty to call evidence at the resumed inquiry which showed I think, from the mouths of half a dozen witnesses that he had accounted for all his movements on the afternoon of the unfortunate day and that he could not have been present on the occasion of Mrs Luard's death. That was the reason I asked the questions, and I thought it was only due to the General and to the public, that the matter, so far as he was concerned, should be absolutely clear in my Court, as there was no other tribunal before which he could give his evidence. Therefore I say that so far as the evidence goes, and we must believe it, he absolutely accounted for all his movements and absolutely showed that he could not have been present and committed this terrible act.

Having finished reviewing the evidence, he turned to the jury and advised them that, 'it is clear that the General could not stand any longer the terrible strain which he was undergoing, and that you can come to no other conclusion than this was a case of suicide. If you feel the intense strain from which he was suffering was enough to unhinge his mind and make him not responsible for his actions, it will be your duty to say that General Luard at the time of his death was not of a sound mind.'

The jury then retired to discuss their finding. After conferring for less than ten minutes they returned a verdict of *suicide while temporarily insane.* The Foreman then passed on behalf of the whole jury, their deep sympathy with Captain Luard and to thank Colonel Warde for his clear and straightforward and explicit statement. The coroner concurred that his lucid statement had greatly helped this inquiry, and they were very much indebted to him.

***

The General's coffin had been placed in the South Lodge pending the funeral and at 9am on the morning of the funeral a hearse pulled by magnificent black shiny horses, the same vehicle that conveyed his wife just a month before, arrived at the lodge and the polished oak coffin was reverently placed in it while Charlie Warde and Elmhirst stood to attention before being driven in a car behind the hearse to the quaint Ightham church where the General had been a church warden. Once again the heavens opened with torrential rain making it a solemn and gloomy atmosphere. It initially appeared that the General's body would be interred in the same weather as his wife's, but luckily it cleared to a sunny day by midday.

The coffin was placed on a trestle in the centre aisle exactly next to the pew the General had worshipped since arriving in the community. Charlie Warde returned with the Captain to the Knoll where the whole extended family had gathered until it was time to attend the service. The road to the tiny church was choked with carriages and cars and many hundreds of residents, drawn by sympathy or out of curiosity, gathered in the precincts of the old parish church, along with dozens of distinguished soldiers and sailors, relatives and friends, all there to pay the last tribute of affection and respect to his memory at the graveside.

They included relatives such as Admiral Sir William Luard, Admiral Patterson, the Reverend Percy Luard and Mr Willink. The friends included the Chief Constable, Mr A Norman the High Sheriff' of Kent, Colonel and Mrs Prevost, Captain Moore, Professor Church. Lady Eleanor and Mary Pratt, Lord Eversley, Canon Horley, Colonel Stockley, Captain Stockley, Major General Goldsworthy, Sir Mark Collett, Major Daniels and Surgeon Major J Ince. It was a veritable Who's Who of County lineage.

A special train had been laid on to transport mourners from London. Edwin and both superintendents were present remaining at a discreet distance. Elmhirst and Mr Hartley drove over from Ightham Knoll in a motor car and were received at the churchyard gates by Charlie Warde. The three men then walked into the church together and took up their places.

Elmhirst was seated on the left side of the aisle and in the second seat from the chancel with the General's brother-in-law Thomas Hartley and next to him Charlie. The rest of the family were sitting opposite. It was noticed that beside Elmhirst on the wall was a tablet in the memory of his brother Eric who had died in Somaliland while serving his country. There were tears in the eyes of most as the sight of the coffin conjured up pictures at what recently occurred with Caroline.

The service began at 3.15pm and surprisingly to many, no military honours were accorded to the dead soldier, and the service both in the church and at the graveside was as simple and brief as possible. Even the singing of a hymn was eliminated from it, as though everyone had experienced enough grief by all the tragedy that had befallen the family. This may have been the wishes of his son who was now the last of a family that just a few weeks ago were all alive, well respected and prominent in local social life. The Reverend B. T. Winnifrith a close friend of the family conducted the service and ended by rather controversially announcing:

> In connection with the tragedies lately enacted in our midst there has been a great lack of charity shown, and many cruel and baseless accusations have been made. There was no doubt that the second tragedy might quite as justly be styled murder as the former one, except that it had taken a far more cruel and harrying form.

The family grave had been reopened by digging right down to his wife's coffin. At the graveside the captain stood where his father had stood when his mother had been buried and like his father was carrying a small bunch of flowers, chrysanthemums this time rather than daisies, his father's favourite flower.

As at the inquest, the most pathetic figure was that of his son and after the funeral ended a silent procession of friends, mostly old and grey-haired colleagues of his father pressed forward to shake his hand. Like a soldier would, he bore himself with fortitude and self-control, but one could not fail to notice that even if he did not dare to show his deep emotion there were many women present who did it for him.

***

In November two months after the murder and suicide the police had by no means abandoned their inquiries and the suicide of his friend had only intensified Warde's frenzied obsession to solve the case and fulfil his promise to the General. He personally posted a reward of £1,000 to anyone who had any information leading to an arrest and prosecution which would end on the 1 January 1909.

This led to a flurry of more claims that kept Edwin and his detectives unnecessarily busy on fool's errands across the County. Naturally, immediately after the murder, everyone was so horrified and dismayed by the tragedy that all classes of the community combined to assist the police in their investigations. But when these investigations bordered on being alarmingly like persecution of innocent people, the community began to turn against the police and was replaced with great resentment.

Warde instructed Edwin's detective department and the whole County force to use any means to find a culprit which one newspaper described as "establishing something akin to a police reign of terror in the district." *The Daily Express* ran a series of articles condemning the Chief Constable for instigating his officers in terrorising inhabitants of the district by their "persistent enquiries."

It was reported that one man, who was "most severely handled," was a very respectable young fellow, the son of a coachman at Seal. Day after day he was put through a most searching cross examination, but naturally being completely innocent, he said nothing which could in any way incriminate him.

It reached a point when any non-resident of the district was accosted and asked his whereabouts on the day of the murder and sometimes detained on very tenuous grounds. Edwin was getting extremely frustrated at the Chief's obsessive behaviour over the case and using his limited manpower on obviously futile investigations when he had so many other urgent cases to deal with. Examples were an unfortunate South African who had returned to visit an elderly couple who had brought him up as a lad in Brasted and was a comparative stranger in the district. Warde and a detective visited him and interrogated him and he admitted he was in the area at the time of the murder but had nothing to do with it. So paranoid was Warde that he got Edwin's detectives to watch his every movement until he eventually conceded that the man was innocent of any crime.

The evening of Friday 13 November proved unlucky for a young man "of colour" according to the *Portsmouth Evening News* when at 6pm as a "consequence of information received" he was detained pending investigations in connection with the Luard murder and taken to Poplar police station in London. Edwin and the Superintendent were informed and unspecified inquiries were made in Sevenoaks and Hull that yet again resulted in nothing, and he was released. In November a youth named Walter Hickey walked into Mill Street police Station in Manchester and gave himself up for the murder saying he used an axe and dagger to kill her.

These investigations spread to London and Manchester and farcically reached the shores of Canada where the Winnipeg correspondent of the *Daily News* reported on 28 November 1908 that a supposed clue to the discovery of the murderer of Mrs Luard, had led the police to commence investigations amongst recent arrivals in the Dominion. Allegedly a detective from Scotland Yard was in Canada engaged in a series of inquiries. Surprise to say the search was fruitless.

And so it continued. Gradually as the months passed public and press interest in the murder waned and dissipated, but Warde had not forgotten.

9

A YEAR LATER – AN ARREST

David Woodruff in the dock

In the thirteen months since the murder the Kent police had kept the case open and remained active in pursuing any leads, due mainly to the Chief Constable's fervour to reclaim some face from the Force's failure in apprehending anyone. It was a question of honour amongst fellow military officers that fuelled his endeavours to catch the perpetrator. And then in September 1909 the Chief Constable finally thought he had got a breakthrough when he was made aware of a man with a history of owning a revolver and threatening people who was in Maidstone prison.

***

David Talbot Woodruff was standing in the queue to enter the casual ward of the Bromley Workhouse at Locks Bottom near Farnborough in Kent. Staying overnight or for longer periods in the workhouse was his way of life but it hadn't always been that way. He had been born in Little Thurlow in Suffolk into a large family and when old enough had joined his father William working as a gardener. He had been good at it and always had work. He got married in 1874 when he was twenty-four to Emma who was from a good family and he was proud of her as she was well educated and spoke six languages, but tragically she died nine years later. He had become a professional gardener and following the death of his wife he moved around the south east managing to work for rich and influential people including Lord Gerrard in Newmarket and at Sandy Bedfordshire.

His work took him to London, and he soon met another lady named Amelia who he married in 1884 in Maida Vale. His business was proving successful, and life was good, but when his second wife died he found life difficult, and his mental health suffered which resulted in him being unable to complete full time work or look after himself. By May 1907 he was living permanently in the Fulham Road workhouse and was a full time vagrant and pauper and looked like one. He had a long greying straggling sandy beard and short hair with a dishevelled tuft on top. His clothes were old and dirty, and his boots muddy and worn. In March 1908, after ten months in the workhouse he headed off and hit the road again wandering as a vagrant and sleeping rough which often got him into trouble with the police who were under recent orders to clamp down on vagrancy.

On one occasion on 13 August 1908, he was in the Sevenoaks area and had lit a fire by the roadside to make a brew when a police officer kicked out his fire and arrested him for sleeping rough. He was put in a cell for the night which actually pleased him. Once released he walked to Tunbridge Wells in search of work and then continued on to Hildenborough managing to find some odd jobs. Then he caught a train to Orpington and later walked to the Bromley workhouse situated in the Kent village of Farnborough. On 24 August, the day of the murder of Mrs Luard, he was in the workhouse and like many others, he had read about her murder. For the next year life continued in the same vein for him wandering from one area to the next staying in workhouses and trying not to overstay his welcome.

Finally on the 13 May 1909 he arrived early back at the Bromley workhouse to be as near to the front of the queue when the doors opened at six as the workhouses were often full if you arrived late. Unbeknown to others in the queue David had secreted in his boot a revolver that had been given to him to look after by a friend he knew at the Fulham Road workhouse but hadn't come back for it. Perhaps foolishly David had hung onto it not knowing what to do with it, but he thought it good for protection as living rough could be a dangerous vocation. It only had one live bullet in it anyway. Although the workhouse normally searched prospective inmates it was only cursory and usually strangely just from the knees up, so he wasn't worried. It was illegal to have a gun of any type without a licence although guns were commonly held by people of all classes, many of them service revolvers from the many wars taking place across the empire.

He got in and settled in the dormitory and next morning the labour master Arthur Bean began to assign jobs to everyone as it wasn't a free ride in these places. David took exception to the job he was given, and a heated argument ensued resulting in a scuffle between the two men. The irate David lost his temper and drew the revolver threatening to shoot Bean. He was arrested and taken to Sevenoaks police station where he was charged with "feloniously attempting to discharge certain loaded arms, to wit, a pistol loaded with gunpowder and a certain leaden bullet, at and against Arthur Bean, with intent to do him grievous bodily harm, at Farnborough, on the 13th. May 1909." He was taken into custody on the 17th. and eventually appeared before the magistrates on the 16th of June when he was found guilty and sentenced to four months hard labour and the gun confiscated.

***

As David's sentence neared its end and his paperwork for release was being prepared, the prison Governor became aware that he had in his care a man who was known to have carried and threatened someone with a revolver and was known to have frequented the Sevenoaks area about the time of the Luard murder. Although the murder of Mrs Luard had occurred over a year before and the manhunt for the culprit had long faded, the Governor became excited. Could he, after all this time, have the guilty party of the most sensational crime of the century sitting in one of his cells? He immediately informed the Chief Constable who became beside himself in the belief that he might at last fulfil the promise to his old comrade.

He immediately contacted Taylor on the matter who wasn't that convinced, but he dispatched Edwin to investigate the possibility, informing him that he had very little time with the release imminent. Having checked the court records of the case edwin visited the Bromley workhouse to interview the staff and then attempted to find out what he could about his previous vagrancy arrest in August 1908, but he still had to try and check David's movements at the time of the Luard murder. Neither Edwin nor Taylor were convinced that he had anything to do with it, but they could not convince Warde who was hell bent on getting him arrested for murder by any means. The day before his release they had little or no evidence to arrest him for murder, but this didn't stop Warde who sent them to Maidstone gaol on his instruction to try and delay his release next day by any subterfuge possible while their boss attempted to get a murder warrant from a magistrate. Prisoners were released officially in the afternoon, but for practical reasons were generally let out at 7am in the morning allowing the staff to prepare the vacated cell for another prisoner and David was expecting this to happen.

On the morning of Saturday 19 September David Talbot Woodruff completed his four-month sentence and was expectantly awaiting his freedom. Several other prisoners were released, but a frustrated David waited impatiently before being informed his release was delayed. They stalled him on the pretext that he was in such a bedraggled state that they would give him special treatment in the form of a better breakfast and that they were obtaining better clothes for him. At lunchtime Taylor had been summoned to Warde's office and handed a warrant for the arrest of Woodruff for the murder of Caroline Luard. Neither he nor Edwin were happy with what was occurring, as Edwin had not found a scrap of evidence to place him at the scene. Taylor in particular, who in normal circumstances would have been the person who applied for the warrant and then presented the case in court, was well aware that he had no concrete evidence to back it up. But he was not unduly surprised that Warde had obtained a warrant as he was close friends with a multitude of magistrates of his class including his brother.

It was 3.15pm when Taylor arrived back at the gaol and the rather confused and frustrated Woodruff was brought to him wanting to know when he was being released only for the superintendent to say:

'I am sorry David I have some bad news for you. I have here a warrant for your arrest for wilfully and feloniously and with malice aforethought murdering Caroline Mary Luard on the 28 September 1908.'

'But I don't understand,' said David, 'I am meant to be released this morning.'

'This is a different charge, nothing to do with what you were in here for.'

'I never did such a thing in my life. I am not guilty of murder or shooting or anything of the kind. I don't know where the place is, and I've never been over there in my life. I know nothing about it.'

Taylor then cautioned him, and with Edwin escorted him to Maidstone train station where they caught a train to Sevenoaks and on to the police station.

***

It wasn't until late evening that news of the arrest leaked out and speedily a crowd collected at the police station and officers placed outside to control them were bombarded with questions. Taylor was accosted by the press as he left the station later and asked if the news of a possible suspect of the murder has been arrested and he replied, 'Quite true. A man has been arrested by me at Maidstone and brought here.'

This statement had reverberations across the country with a renewed press frenzy and resurrected all the rumour-mongering yet again. Two days later on Monday 21 September 1909 to David's bewilderment he found himself before the magistrates at the small Sevenoaks police court in front of Mr Crosbie-Hill the Chairman along with the Reverend John Jackson and four others. Mr W House of solicitors Messrs Neve and House of Sevenoaks and Tonbridge represented him, and the Chief Constable prosecuted. Warde had positioned himself at the back in the shadows of the court to watch the poor superintendent try and make the best of the case. Understandably Taylor was not a happy man. The courthouse was packed as there had been understandably great excitement over the weekend. Reporters and photographers had swarmed to the town.

At 11.15am the sixty-three-year-old ex-gardener David Talbot Woodruff of no fixed abode was charged with the wilful murder of Mrs Luard on the night of August 24, 1908. He tottered into the dock escorted by the lockup constable to great disappointment. He was not the ruffian of terrible fierceness that the crowds in the court had anticipated, but according to the *Morning Reader* correspondent was "a shrivelled old gentleman with a rheumy eye and a countenance scared into sheer bewilderment. A tuft of hair reared itself comically over his tall white forehead for all the world like the crest of a cockatoo, and a shade of weariness passed over his almost expressionless face."

He was dressed in a faded grey tweed jacket suit, cotton shirt and dirty boots and with a straggling sandy beard tinged with grey, and short hair he appeared to be a harmless old tramp. His right hand nervously clutched the front rail of the dock while his left pulled aimlessly at his straggly beard while he stood throughout the proceedings which he followed intently.

Taylor told the court that on Saturday, 18 September he received a warrant for the arrest of the prisoner who was in Maidstone Prison on another charge. He saw him there at 3pm and asked him, 'Is your name David Woodruff?' He replied yes and I told him, 'I have a warrant for your arrest, and I must caution you that anything you may say will be given in evidence against you. I then read the warrant to him as follows: that on the 24th of August, in the year 1908, at the Parish of Seal, in the county of Kent, you feloniously, wilfully, and with malice aforethought, did kill and murder one, Mary Caroline Luard, against the peace of our Sovereign Lord the King, his Crown and dignity.'

On the train journey from Maidstone to Sevenoaks Woodruff said, "I don't know where the parish of Seal is. I have never been there in my life, and I know nothing about it." When we arrived at Sevenoaks Police Station I formally charged him, and he made no reply.'

Mr House, for the defence asked Taylor, 'At what time did you receive the warrant?'

'I think about noon on Saturday.'

'Did you know how it was that the prisoner happened to be at Maidstone gaol?'

'I believe he was there on another charge.'

'Had his sentence ended?'

'I believe so.'

'When?'

'I expect on that day, some time, the ordinary practice being to discharge the prisoners in the early morning. I really could not tell you about the procedure.'

'Do you know why he was detained?'

'No.'

'Do you know on what evidence this warrant was issued?'

'No.'

'You say you are not familiar with the practice of discharging prisoners?'

'I am not.'

'Superintendent Taylor, on this evidence I cannot believe you are asking for a remand for a week?'

Taylor then addressed the bench saying, 'That is all the evidence I propose to offer, and I would ask that the prisoner be remanded for a week for further inquiries.'

An incredulous and incensed Mr House said in response, 'I shall oppose that application. It seems to me that the police, for some reason best known to themselves, but unknown to anybody else, arrested this man upon suspicion, thirteen months after this offence. They arrest a man in Maidstone prison, who is there on an ordinary trifling charge of common assault. They take proceedings against him and try to make a case against him. I feel so strongly about this matter that I am afraid of making some indiscretion in addressing the Bench. There is no reason why there should be a remand, and if I go too far, perhaps you will stop me. I feel the case should never have been brought before the court. The police have had thirteen months in which to find the man guilty of this offence, an offence, of course, we all deplore, and would be only too pleased to find the guilty party. The only reason is, so far as I can make out, is that at some time or other he had a revolver in his possession. Although he was only in prison for a common assault, his clothes were several times searched while he was in there and they took his own clothes from him when he was being discharged from prison, his own clothes have been withheld from him and he is wearing others. He has been four months in prison and the police have not even now a shred of evidence against him. They had him more than enough time in which to work up a case against him and yet they have the cheek to ask for a week's remand to endeavour to give evidence against him. Surely some evidence should be given now to show on what grounds the warrant was issued, some evidence to justify the arrest?'

The chairman asked Mr House, 'Do you say he has been in prison for four months?'

'Yes, for an assault.'

'Did you say it was a trifling offence?'

'It may have been a serious one, but that is not my point. For four months the police have made their enquiries and found nothing, and do not intend to give any today.'

Poor Taylor, who was aware that Warde was eyeing him keenly, interposed at this point and said, 'Although the man has been imprisoned for four months, the facts have only recently come to our knowledge upon which we wish to make further enquiries.'

The Chairman asked Taylor, 'Is there any further evidence forthcoming today?'

'No, sir.'

The Chairman, after consulting with his colleagues announced, 'the bench are of the opinion that this is hardly sufficient evidence to justify us in remanding this man and we ought to have had further evidence presented to us today.'

Warde, realising that the proceedings were not going his way stepped forward at this point and asked to address the bench to try and rescue the situation. He began to speak but was interrupted by Mr House who turned to the bench and asked, 'Surely if the Chief Constable wishes to speak he should do it from the witness box and be sworn in?'

The chairman agreed, and Warde marched to the box glowering at the defence lawyer and said, 'It is only within the last week that certain facts have come to my knowledge that have caused inquiries to be made. Therefore we are naturally anxious to have a remand.'

The chairman replied, 'As I have already ruled, in the bench's opinion, more evidence would be necessary to justify this remand.'

Warde retorted, 'Certain statements which have been made are not quite accurate. The prisoner was asked by the governor of Maidstone prison if he had any objection to his clothes being taken away and he said no.'

The chairman was beginning to get exasperated and demanded, 'Are you prepared to bring forth further evidence today?'

'Not today, sir. Of course I can give certain facts within my own knowledge which caused me to have the prisoner arrested, but I should be very loathe to do that. The hands of the police are very much tied, and we want to make certain inquiries before we can make public what we have in our possession.'

The magistrates then retired again and on returning into court after about three minutes, the chairman said, 'The bench are of the opinion that there is not sufficient evidence to warrant us in ordering this man's detention. He will, therefore, be liberated.'

A rather dazed and confused Woodruff was having trouble comprehending what was happening and lingered in the dock until an official guided him away to the accompaniment of loud cheers and clapping from the crowded court, given in sympathy for the victim of what most of them viewed as a gross blunder by the Kent Police. Outside the crowd smiled and wagged their heads wisely and the news was spread all over town in five minutes. It was almost unheard of for a decision to be given in deliberate opposition to the request of a Chief Constable. The press described the proceedings as "little short of farcical" stating Woodruff was arrested under a cloak of secrecy and handed the charge of murder without a single piece of evidence brought to justify the serious accusation. Taylor and Edwin, showing what compassion they could, took him into the police canteen and gave him a substantial meal and copious tea.

'We would strongly advise in order to avoid the press and cameras outside to wait a little longer until they disperse,' advised Edwin.

'I would rather get away now if you will allow.'

'Of course, but best to leave by the back door just in case.'

'That would be kind of you,'

'Where are you headed now?'

'I'm getting out of here and going to London.'

With that he was shown out and walked through Knowle Park heading for the railway station. He did not completely avoid the press as one reporter managed to get an interview. When asked about his arrest for murder he commented:

> I certainly did not expect the arrest. I know absolutely nothing about the case, and I don't even know where Mrs Luard lived or anything about her. On the date of the murder I was in Farnborough. I have not always been, as I am now, tramping about and getting an odd job as a gardener here and there. I had a revolver with me when I was arrested at Bromley four months ago, but it was not mine. It was left with me by a friend while he went abroad, I don't know of my own knowledge, but I am told that the revolver has been examined by the police experts and it was found to be of a different calibre to the bullets discovered in Mrs Luard's body.

David returned to London and continued his vagrant lifestyle taking bricklaying and gardening jobs when he felt able to, but his health and well-being was deteriorating. His main haunt was the Westminster workhouse in Fulham Road until on the 9 December 1911 his behaviour and mental capacity was so poor he was admitted to the Bansted lunatic asylum where he remained until his death on 27 June 1915.

10

THE AFTERMATH

Every part of the Luard family tragedy upset and enraged Edwardian society. The murder of Mrs Luard, and the suicide of her husband, the anonymous hoaxes and malicious letters and telegrams, the wrongful arrest of Woodruff, the perceived incompetence of the police and their failure in apprehending the culprit, the behaviour of the press and the conduct of the Chief Constable all came under scrutiny and were complained about. The question of the venomous letters which led to the General's death and on which Thomas Buss had vented his anger at the inquest was for most people the most disturbing aspect.

Emotions were running high after the General's suicide particularly amongst his influential friends who believed he was "done to death by slanderous tongues" and they wanted revenge. The Reverend B T Winnifrith probably summed up the feeling best when he said at the funeral "there was no doubt that the second tragedy might quite as justly be styled murder as the former one, except that it had taken a far more cruel and harrying form."

At the first Malling Court petty session after the suicide where the General once sat on the bench, and where all his colleagues were close friends, Mr Robert Norton, the Chairman that day, took the unusual step of reading the following statement in support of their late colleague:

> Since the court last met, we have lost under the most tragic circumstances, our respected colleague General Luard. The whole of the details connected with the death of Mrs Luard and the General are too harrowing to be dwelt upon here. But our respect and most respectful sympathies go out to Captain Luard and his relatives in their bereavement. Those of us who knew General Luard intimately have been terribly shocked by many of the circumstances which have surrounded the case, more particularly by the deliberate, unscrupulous and venomous attacks which were made upon him by anonymous letter writers unsupported by any particle of evidence. It is sincerely to be hoped that steps may be taken, if possible, under the guidance and supervision of the Home Office, to carry out the suggestion of the coroner and jury with a view to the detection and punishment of the authors of these anonymous letters.

The statement was signed by his fellow magistrates Mr Robert Norton. Sir Mark Collet, Lord Arthur Butler, Major General Goldsworthy, Colonel Luck, Colonel Stockley, Mr. Lee Smith, and Mr W Wigan.

Even the Lord Chief Justice, Lord Alverstone, felt he had to speak out and when he addressed a dinner of the Sphinx Club at the magnificent Cecil Hotel London in February 1909, his speech mentioned the General stating "the unfortunate man who I know was absolutely innocent was driven to death by publicity and by anonymous letters." He went on to condemn the craze of so-called "smart people for seeing their names in the paper."

It wasn't just the judiciary calling for the punishment of the authors of the letters, but the Luard family as well. Mr Thomas Winter Kennion, Caroline's nephew, wrote to the *People* and the letter was published in their Sunday, October 4, issue. In it he pleaded:

> that some means should be found whereby these pests can be dealt with. At the present moment, it would almost seem that anyone of us who may, by unusual circumstances, beheld in the public eye is open to the frenzied attacks of any maniac or criminal who can afford to pay for a penny stamp. It is to be supposed that among a population so large as that of Great Britain there must exist under insufficient control a large number of more or less unsound minds, and it is no doubt from these people, and from the so-called religious hysteria maniacs that the letters have mostly come. The fact remains that by the abuse of our postal system, these wretches are able to inflict their venomous wounds on anyone who comes within their ken. But apart from this on public grounds and for the safety of any man among us who may be laid open to these shall attacks, I would urge that the Home Office should deal severely with those who have used our Postal Service for such infamous purpose.

The arrest of Woodruff on a charge of murder by the Chief Constable of Kent without producing any evidence to justify the accusation caused severe criticism in many quarters and reached a point when the press and judiciary were calling for his resignation. Feelings were running high throughout the county for weeks after the trial. It became a sensation and disturbed both the public and the judiciary because it was almost unheard of for a court to refuse a request from a Chief Constable to remand a prisoner.

It was headlined a police blunder by the media. It had infuriated Mr House, his solicitor, so much that he began making complaints about the treatment of his client in high places. This was mainly aimed at the Chief Constable who was to have a few weeks of intense discomfort. House first complained to Mr Edward Pickersgill, Liberal Member of Parliament for Bethnal Green in London who took an interest in criminal law particularly murder cases and the abolition of the death penalty. It was noted that House did not approach the local M.P. who was of course the Chief Constable's brother. Mr Pickersgill, like House, believed that the rights of Woodruff had been impinged and that he should never have been charged. He brought the matter up in the House of Commons on Monday 27 September and asked Mr Gladstone, the Home Secretary whether in the ordinary course his client should have been entitled to be discharged on or about seven o'clock in the morning and under what authority and by whose order he was detained until three o'clock in the afternoon when he was charged with murder.

Mr Masterman, Under Secretary to the Home Office, later replied that a prisoner is not entitled to his discharge until the end of the day on which his sentence expires. As a matter of convenience, prisoners are normally discharged early in the day, but circumstances often occur which make it desirable to detain a prisoner till a later hour. The prison authorities acted at the request of the Chief Constable for the execution of the warrant. The Home Secretary's opinion was that they would have been wrong had they released him, knowing that he was wanted by the police on a charge of murder. He stated the police were not under his control but that of the Chief Constable and the Standing Joint Committee of Kent.

There was worse to come for the Chief Constable when Rev. John Jackson, one of the magistrates on the case, waded in and issued a statement to the press:

> I feel very strongly that this charge should never have been before us in that form. My fellow magistrates and I were unanimously of the opinion that such a case could not be supported for a moment without a particle of evidence. I think there should be a very full enquiry into the action of the Chief Constable of Kent, on whose sworn information the warrant was originally granted. On such a charge, that of wilful murder, the most serious that can be brought against any man, when his life and liberty are in grave danger, the upmost care and caution should be exercised by superior officials to avoid any suspicion of injustice or high-handed action. The question is of the utmost public importance, involving, as it does, the whole liberty of the subject and the right of every one of us to fair treatment, even in the face of suspicion, which may be and often is groundless.

A special correspondent of another morning paper with long experience of the mysterious actions of the authorities in the application of criminal law wrote:

> I can call to mind no parallel with the case of the unfortunate gardener David Woodruff, who lived a torturing ten minutes in the dock before the Justices took a sensible and humane course, the only course possible under the circumstances to set him free. After consultation in their private room, which lasted just three minutes, they firmly and unanimously rule in direct opposition to the urgent request

> of Lieutenant Colonel Warde, the Chief Constable of Kent. The decision was quite clear and quite condemnatory in a sentence. It was a unanimous vote of no confidence in the gentleman who is the head of the police of their county. I understand there was nothing in the sworn information to justify either Colonel Warde's demand for a remand or even Woodruff's arrest. It was generally agreed that the magistrate's action was remarkable and unprecedented.After having brought disaster upon failure by arresting a poor man with not even a shadow of a suspicion against him and charging him with the gravest offence in the criminal catalogue, the general opinion in this district is that the best thing, Lieutenant Colonel Warde can do is to place his resignation in the hands of the Standing Joint Committee.

In an interview, Lieutenant Colonel Warde replied to some of the criticisms which had been levelled against the County police authorities with regard to the arrest of Daniel Woodruff. He stated:

> The action I took was justified by the circumstances at the time. That is all I can say. If no person was ever arrested on suspicion, few criminals will be detected at all and hardly any crime will be solved. The magistrate who granted the warrant and the Clerk to the justices knew these circumstances privately from me before I swore the information on which to launch it. I must confess I was surprised at the action of the magistrates, for it is usual to leave a matter of this kind to the discretion of the Chief Constable, whose hands are tied because he is not always in a position to state all he knows at the time. The difficulties of anyone at the

> head of any criminal investigation are naturally great. And this case has been a particularly delicate and difficult task from the first. We are still doing our upmost to solve this most complicated case and our only desire is to find the right man without doing any injustice to the innocent.

***

This particular case, unlike any others before, caused great consternation in the public, the press and even within the Kent Constabulary itself over the general safety and policing of the county. In particular whether the police had the capacity to keep the county safe. This concern was mostly prompted by those of higher status as Caroline was one of their "own" making it more outrageous and worrying in their eyes.

At the time of the murder the force was inadequately equipped and trained to patrol 1,368 square miles of territory and 350 miles of coastline and look after just over half a million residents with its 550 officers. It was 1919 before the constables were issued with such useful pieces of equipment such as an electric torch. Amazingly it was 1931 before sixteen motorcycles and one car was acquired so that motorised patrols could be introduced.

The press took the opportunity to highlight this growing anxiety caused by Caroline's murder and some commentators could not resist the perennial jibe of the police wasting time on unimportant crime instead of dealing with the perceived threat of increasing vagrancy:

> We hold very strongly to the view that a searching inquiry ought to be made into the strength and sufficiency of our county constabulary. This is not a moment, perhaps, to emphasise the vulgar charge that the police are too busy setting motor traps to fulfil their primary duty of perambulat-

ing the countryside. But outside the large towns there is a growing conviction that the police force has not kept pace, either in numbers or intelligence, with the increase of population, and especially with the growth of "masterless" men the sturdy vagabonds of Tudor Legislation, (a reference to a stringent series of laws dating back to the 1601 Elizabethan Poor Law aimed to deter vagrancy and poverty, but did not address the root causes) who infest the main roads, and who are a terror and a nuisance alike to the pedestrian and the cottager. The police force is barely adequate for ordinary patrol work, and any sudden demand upon them will leave whole districts unprotected. And every winter sees a "burglar scare" only too well founded in villaindom. We want more judges like Sir Alfred Lawrence, who has put the fear of God into the bullies and blackguards of Cardiff. And we want the Home Secretary who will be proof to those petitions for reprieve, some of which are scarcely less criminal than the actions which have set them in motion.

Henry Warde, the Chief Constable, survived all the criticism against him and the call for his resignation and completed another thirteen years retiring in June 1921. In fairness to him, he did his best within the financial constraints and lack of technology to introduce innovations and improve conditions for the officers during his tenure.

The Wilkinson's, having boarded up the Casa decided to demolish it as they felt they could never use it again after the terrible event, but for reasons not known the demolition never took place and the building was left to slowly deteriorate until it collapsed leaving just the concrete base.

A new tenant was found for the Ightham Knoll by the name of Berthold Brown who moved in during January 1909 not realising the draw the house had on morbid sightseers even a year after the events. There was a constant stream of unwanted visitors wandering up to the house and into the grounds to stand and gawk which obviously became a nuisance forcing him to write a letter to the *Sevenoaks Chronicle* on 1 October 1909 expressing his grievances:

> Sir, I venture to ask if the Knoll, Ightham, may now be given a rest? I am tenant since January of the house and am constantly annoyed by numerous calls and letters from inquisitive visitors. I wish to point out that the tragedy was not committed in my house or on the grounds, but about two miles away, and the public will see as little in or about the house to interest their morbid curiosity as if they went to Dum-Dum in India.

11

WHODUNNIT?

So whodunnit? As mentioned in the prologue I have not discovered the identity of the assailant but have endeavoured to pursue a different angle to the story by putting it into the context of the social history of the time and the ramifications to everyone involved. It soon became obvious to the police early on that it was unsolvable but investigations continued mainly because of the Chief Constable's obsession with his promise to his friend Charles to find his wife's murderer. Conspiracy theorists have probably spent too much time in their attempts to make more of the story than it was. As a fourteenth century logician and theologian Friar William of Ockham apparently once said, "the simplest answer is almost always the best one" and this is undoubtedly true in this case.

There have been endless theories and written accounts over the decades and one incongruity that has bothered many people is why the General and Caroline left it so late to take the fatal walk that afternoon when they both knew a visitor was expected at about 4.30pm especially as Caroline allegedly intended lingering there to take in the view. There was also the question of why the idea that the crime could have been committed by an itinerant of some kind was mostly discounted early on in the investigation.

The divide between rich and poor was as great in the affluent rural areas of Kent as it was in the cities. Workhouses and lunatic asylums were also just as prevalent and in most cases full to overflowing. Crime was quite high mainly due to London villains arriving daily much to the angst of Edwin Fowle and his colleagues, particularly jewel thieves to burgle and loot the big country houses and to defraud, commit violence and pick pockets. As already mentioned the situation was made worse every summer and early autumn with the arrival of economic drifters and pickers, not necessarily all honest and despite the police regularly moving these people on, large numbers slept in the woods, fields, haystacks and barns, derelict farm buildings and houses; and often fought between themselves.

Most residents had guns in their possession not just shotguns or rifles, but hand guns as well. Like the General they kept them in their houses at strategic points to combat any burglars who dared to invade their property and many were military men who knew how to use them. This was an indication of the perceived threat these vagrants posed and the newspapers picked up on this tension and frustration and wrote many columns on the subject while the residents such as the General wrote indignant letters about it.

So in this context many doubted the wisdom of Caroline to regularly wander the woods alone but her long acquaintance with the locality and its people had made her confident of her safety and removed any fears of molestation. She also would have been well aware of the many itinerant persons who in the summertime were present in great numbers and it was common knowledge that she was anything but a nervous woman. There is no doubt that had she come across anyone committing a misdemeanour such as breaking into the Casa for shelter or to burgle she would no doubt have accosted them.

Any consideration that Caroline was shot purely through a chance encounter with a surprised would-be robber or burglar was put on the back burner as the scenario seemed inconceivable that a petty thief, vagrant or seasonal worker would own or have in his possession a gun or be desperate enough or violent enough to use it. But guns were readily available and incredibly cheap to buy with many service pieces circulating brought back from the numerous conflicts across the empire over the last decades such as the Boer wars. Mr Churchill, the gun expert, had at the inquest admitted that guns were available for as little as a pound. David Woodruff was a prime example of this.

There is also a social and economic context to be considered that summer and early autumn of 1908 in Kent. According to newspaper reports, the unseasonal heavy rain and gales had plagued the area for weeks interfering with the annual hop and fruit picking. The *Whitstable Times* reported on the 5 September that:

> the hop pickers are in a pitiable plight. In addition to a lack of employment, they have had to endure the discomfort of relentless rain and having little or no means, they find themselves on the *verge of starvation*. The heavy winds and blinding rainstorms have done very extensive damage in the gardens, and acres of hops are lying on the ground.

Other newspapers reported that some pickers were in a very sorry plight and a few had returned home while those that remained were desperate enough to have accepted pitiful payments for their endeavours. The dramatic assertion that people were on the verge of starvation makes it more conceivable that it may have led to one of them to be desperate enough to have attempted to rob Caroline as although the rings wrenched from her fingers and her purse torn from her pocket may not have been of "great" value" to some there worth would be immense to a desperate penniless vagrant or worker. All this gives more credence to a chance robbery by a desperate man being the motive rather than "a villain of not only exceptional brutality, but cunning" as one newspaper reported.

So is it so far-fetched to accept that the simple explanation was that a variety of unfortunate chance events put Caroline in the presence of an armed violent thief or a desperate itinerant intending to break into the Casa and suffered the consequences of her possibly noble intervention. It is no more bizarre than any of the other conspiracy theories and possible proof that the "simplest answer is almost always the best one."

Alamy photo

12

WHO WAS EDWIN FOWLE?

Edwin Fowle is the central character in *The Edwardian Detective Edwin Fowle Series* of books for good reason as he was a much acclaimed and respected police officer in his time with an exemplary and extraordinary career, but like many of his ilk has been forgotten by history. His time as a detective spanned exactly the Edwardian era and during his 42 years and 3 months loyal service to the Kent County Constabulary he was awarded many accolades collecting a police merit star and over twenty commendations.

His police career spanned the reigns of four monarchs, and he experienced the emergence of motor vehicles, extensive train lines, telephones, radio, major advances in forensic science and innovations in policing methods as well as social transformations and changes in criminal behaviour which he seems to have taken all in his stride managing to adapt to all the new challenges. He was always viewed as a rising star and rose through the ranks from a lowly constable in October 1890 to Superintendent in charge of his own division in 1911.

He was five feet nine inches tall, broad shouldered and of stout stature with a well-groomed large moustache below a substantial nose. He was described as a driven and religious man with a great sense of duty, a somewhat questioning mind and a tenacious nature, perfect attributes for a detective. He was a stickler for correct police procedure and record keeping and his superiors and the judiciary were complimentary for the way he prepared cases for court, few of which failed to get a prosecution. As a detective he was always smartly dressed, always wearing a fashionable derby hat and overcoat.

Born in 1872 to Thomas and Margaret in the small village of Preston situated between Canterbury and Ramsgate he became part of a family police dynasty as his father Thomas was also a celebrated Kent policeman who surpassed Edwin by completing 53 years' service and rose to the rank of superintendent. Two of Edwin's three brothers were Kent police officers. His elder brother Thomas rose to the rank of superintendent and his younger brother Ivo was an Inspector and one of his uncles was in the police before becoming a railway detective. They managed to boast three superintendents and an inspector in the family with an unrivalled combined service record of 165 years excluding the uncle.

He worked as a cooper in the village until he was eighteen and old enough to join. During his first six years he was posted to the Kentish towns of Gillingham, Westgate, Dartford, Ightham and Malling where he gained considerable experience. There was no real training at the time, and he learned from his father and other "old hands." From the beginning he was perceived as having a natural aptitude for police work and particularly an ability for investigative work.

So when on the 1 July 1896 the Force had the prescience to establish a detective branch at their Wrens Court headquarters in Maidstone he was immediately picked to become one of the first three detective constables in the history of the force under the supervision of one Detective Sergeant. This tiny unit was responsible for serious crime across the County, and he helped launch and shape this new innovation. He made such an impression that four years later in 1900 he was promoted to First Class Detective Sergeant and was put in charge of the department.

In the next six years he made quite a name for himself becoming one of the most recognised officers across the County although he made every effort to shun the press and publicity and never gave interviews he was ever in the newspapers due to the many headline cases he investigated. This resulted in him attaining another record when on 1 February 1906 he was promoted the first Detective Inspector in the history of the Kent County Constabulary. He was a popular officer and familiar to most of the public, judiciary, local authorities, coroners, his far-flung colleagues across the County, also to many villains. He was called upon to deal with every known class of crime whether it be murder, fraud, infanticide, robbery, hotel theft, housebreaking or pickpocketing. He was sadly regularly engaged in investigating child murders prevalent in his early years which were distressing for him as a religious man.

His pet hate were all the London pick-pocket gangs that frequented Kent which he pursued with a vengeance. One of his attributes was that he never forgot a face. He made a point of knowing them and they soon knew him, some of them to their cost. Such was his fixation that he could recognise all the members of the leading notorious London and Kent pickpocket gangs. Despite this the criminal fraternity had a wary respect for him and referred to him as "The Pickpocket Terror."

While a detective between 1900-1911 he collected many commendations and awards. The most memorable being three headline murder cases; known as The Tonbridge murder (1901), The Tenterden Murder (1905) and the Seal Chart Murder (1908). For the Tonbridge and Tenterden murders he received a commendation from the Director of Public Prosecutions (DPP) and the Chief Constable and for the Tenterden murder a police Merit Star. These three murders are all part of my *Detective Edwin Fowle Series.*

He was married on the 9th. November 1910 in St Michaels Church, Beckenham to Annie Sophia Vockins. Edwin remained with the detective department until his promotion on the 20 April 1911 to the rank of Superintendent. He was given command of the Sevenoaks Division, "a post which he held with zeal from that day" until his retirement in December 1932. While in Sevenoaks he was known for his patience and tact and "preventing frayed tempers."

He was highly respected by the public, counsel, solicitors, magistrates and local authorities and loved by his men; encouraging them in their recreations especially cricket and rifle shooting and tutored them in first aid. Under his guidance his men played a conspicuous part assisting the injured in the disastrous 1927

Sevenoaks train crash which killed thirteen people. On retirement he remained in Sevenoaks. He was also an animal lover.

He died peacefully aged 73 in Holmesdale Hospital Sevenoaks in 1944 and was buried in Greatness cemetery. At his funeral the vicar spoke of the power by which he had lived and served the police force. First there was the sense of duty by which he was always exact, ready and alert to execute his work and secondly there was the maintenance of peace inspired by the source of all power, God.

The funeral was attended by family, dozens of senior officers from across the County, as well as rank and file and a large contingent of local dignitaries, friends, acquaintances and towns folk and even the local RSPCA Inspector.

13

BIBLIOGRAPHY

SELECTED REFERENCES

Over 150 articles were researched in the British Newspaper Archives (BNA) and the following are a selection. All newspapers 1908 unless otherwise annotated.

General Story

Sevenoaks Chronicle Fri 28 August, Shocking Tragedy at Seal Chart p8

Sevenoaks Chronicle, 4 September 4. The Seal Chart Murder p5 & 8

The Courier, 28 August, Murder at Ightham Knoll, p9

Sevenoaks Chronicle & Kentish Advertiser, August 28 Shocking tragedy at Seal Chart. p3

Tuesday

Lloyd's Weekly News, 30 August , Mysterious Murder in Summerhouse, p5

Reynolds Newspaper, Sunday, September 20, Fruitless Digging Operations

Morning Post Tuesday 1 September. Murder of Mrs Luard. Singular Development. p 5

Kentish Advertiser Friday 11 September, The Chief Detectives Experiments

The Courier, 4 September 4, Case Reconstructed p5

The Morning Post, 1 September Murder of Mrs Luard, a Singular development p5

Inquest

Sevenoaks Chronicle and Kentish Advertiser Friday, September 4 Some revolver test. p5.

Sevenoaks Chronicle & Kentish Advertiser Fri September 11 p8 Mr Churchill Describes Fatal Bullets.

The Globe, 5th Evening Edition, Thursday 27 August The Excluded Press.

The Free Press September 4 The Sevenoaks Murder p3 (Yellow car)

The Globe Wednesday, September 30. 1908, Elmhirst's letter p6.

Weekly Dispatch, Sunday 30 August Pathetic Scenes at Funeral p1

Wasted Time

The Morning Post, Wednesday 2 September, Failure of Every Clue p6

The Globe Thursday September 3,Supposed Valuable Clue Man's Strange Behaviour near Maidstone.p7

Portsmouth Evening News Saturday, November 14, A Negro Detained p5.

Lloyds Weekly News Human Bloodhound September 8 wed p5

Lloyd's Weekly News September 13 Human Bloodhound p5

Morning Post. Wednesday 26 August, Searching the Woods for a Clue. p5

The Western Herald, 25 September 1909, Arrested on Suspicion, Severely handled.

Whodunnit?

Whitstable Times and Herne Bay Herald, Saturday 5, Hop Pickers Plight p7.

The Tragedy

The People, Sunday 20 September Suicide of General Luard, p6

The Daily Mail Saturday. Last Moment Tragedy of Generals Despair.

Sevenoaks Chronicle Friday September 25 Distressing Affair on the Line p8

Maidstone Journal & Kentish Advertiser 24 September, The Luard tragedy p3

The People Sunday 20 September, Suicide of Genera Luard p6

Kent and Sussex Courier Friday 25 September, Capt. Luards return p8.

Reynolds Newspaper, Sun 20 September, Furniture Sold at Auction

T*he Western Herald* 28 November, Ruminant Canadian Clue.

The Courier, 25 September, A Servant and General Luard

A Year Later

The Globe Mon 20 September, An Arrest Maidstone p7

Reynold's Newspaper Sunday 26 September 26, 1909, Innocent Man Arrested. Police Blunder p3

Lloyd's Weekly News, 26 September 1909, Garner Arrested, p11.

Aftermath

The East Kent Gazette Sat Oct 2 Magistrate and Chief Constable interviewed.

Maidstone Journal September 30, 1909, Questions in Parliament p7

London Evening Standard, Tuesday 21 September 1909, Law and Police p7

People. Sunday, October 4, Remarkable letter from a relative

Morning Leader Friday 22 October 1909 P5 Home Office Decision

OTHER SOURCES

Kent Police 1857-1957.Centenary Booklet, Edited by R.L.Thomas (1957.)

Census 1901, 1911

National Archives

Ancestry.com

British Newspaper Archive, BNA.

Wikipedia.org

FURTHER READING

Percy Savage, Savage of Scotland Yard, Hutchnson & Co, London p88-99

Diane James, Edwardian Murder, The History Press, 2009

Sir Sidney Orme Rowan-Hamilton, The Trial of John Alexander Dickman (1914).

Minette Walters, A Dreadful Murder Pan Books, London, 2013.

John Brookland, Case Histories of a Real Edwardian Detective, Bitzabooks, (2025)

John Brookland, The Tonbridge Outrage, Bitza Books, (2024)

John Brookland

ABOUT THE AUTHOR

John Brookland is now retired and lives in Suffolk, U.K. after a long-varied career working at the sharp end of animal welfare in the U.K and abroad. Having always had an interest in social history and true crime he now researches and writes books and magazine articles on these subjects. These include the Detective Edwin

Fowle series chronicling the exploits of a real celebrated Edwardian detective. He has also authored memoirs of his work helping animals in the U.K. and abroad and books on the history of department stores and the War Horses.

He has a popular educational animal welfare blog and website https://www.animalrightsandwrongs.uk. commentating on international and U.K. animal issues with readers in over 70 countries. When not writing he enjoys travelling with his partner Debbie to exotic places to view wildlife and hiking the U.K. countryside.

Find out more on the author's website: www.bitzabooks.co.uk

THE EDWARDIAN DETECTIVE EDWIN FOWLE SERIES

The Tonbridge Outrage
The Tenterden Murder
Murder in Seal Chart
Det. Edwin Fowle Investigates

Other True Crime
The Madness of Bertha Peterson

Published by bitzabooks.co.uk

www.ingramcontent.com/pod-product-compliance
Lightning Source LLC
LaVergne TN
LVHW050821061126
851857LV00012B/907